CAMPERVAN CRAZY

CAMPERVAN

TRAVELS WITH MY BUS: A TRIBUTE TO THE VW CAMPER AND THE PEOPLE WHO DRIVE THEM

KYLE BOOKS

CRAZY

DAVID AND CEE ECCLES

This book is dedicated to our children, Hal, Ceri and Hollie, who grew up with our passion.

This paperback edition first published in Great Britain in 2015 by Kyle Books, an imprint of Kyle Cathie Ltd.
192–198 Vauxhall Bridge Road
London, SW1V 1DX
general.enquiries@kylebooks.com
www.kylebooks.com

First published in hardback in 2006 by Kyle Cathie Ltd.

10 9 8 7 6 5 4 3 2 1

ISBN: 978 0 85783 313 6

Editorial director Muna Reyal
Designer Geoff Hayes
Copy editor Alison Wormleighton
Production Sha Huxtable and Alice Holloway

David and Cee Eccles are hereby identified as the authors of this work in accordance with Section 77 of the Copyright, Designs and Patents Act 1988.

A Cataloguing in Publication record for this title is available from the British Library.

Colour reproduction by Sang Choy.
Printed and bound in China by Toppan Leefung Printing Ltd.

CONTENTS

INTRODUCTION

This book celebrates the Volkswagen camper and the people who drive and love this unique vehicle. It is not a historical account of the development of a classic design icon, nor is it an information or fact book. This is well documented in many other titles. Rather, it is the bringing together and sharing of a passion enjoyed by many, and a tribute to the diversity of owners and their obsession with something that is central to their lives and a loved family member: the VW campervan, in all its guises.

OBSESSION OR ADDICTION?

It has been over sixty years since the humble, no-frills VW Transporter was first introduced, and it is now more popular than ever. Quite why this is so is difficult to explain, but no other vehicle engenders such warm affection or is so central to the lives of its owners. VW campers and buses now command very high prices and are highly sought after.

They symbolise fun, freedom and adventure and are frequently used in advertising campaigns and films to project lifestyle images. Although the vehicles are often associated with surfers or hippies, the truth is that VW owners are an eclectic mix of all ages and backgrounds who share a common passion – the love of their bus. They flash their lights and wave at each other using the 'wiggle wave' of thumb and little finger, which forms a VW shape, based on the old surfers' 'hang-loose wave'. They gather in their thousands at special events and shows where they talk for hours about their own pride and joy and admire what others have done to their vans. They fit big engines to them and race them on drag strips. They strap surfboards to the roof and head off to the nearest beach. They gather in groups at campsites for weekends away from the hurly-burly of daily life. Some undertake epic journeys round Europe or across Africa, Asia, or the Americas; others use them for shorter holidays with the family. They use them for load-hauling and for moving house. They spend countless hours and money maintaining them. They design, adapt and create their own interiors to suit their lifestyle. Some customise them and paint them to create their own individual look; others painstakingly restore them to original condition.

VW buses are slow, they struggle up hills and they need constant attention, but that is part of the appeal – the journey is just as important as the destination. With a VW campervan you can stop where you want and when you want, without the need to find a hotel or place to eat. It's your living room, bedroom, restaurant – the famous window sticker that reads 'Home is where you park it' says it all. The campervan makes you part of a romantic dream harking back to a time when life was much simpler. It allows you to meet new friends, sleep in wild places, travel off the beaten track and decide where tomorrow will take you. It gives you the chance to be individuals in a world of clones and package holidays and watch the sun go down and decide where tomorrow will take you.

Campervan owners love their buses as if they were living things. Some buses are deemed female, some male. Nearly every bus is given a name by its owners, and choosing a name for your bus is an important initiation rite for a new owner. In a world of sophisticated technology, MPVs and 4x4s, where the car you drive is an important status symbol, it seems paradoxical that the upsurge of interest in the VW bus shows no signs of abating and the number on the roads seems to grow.

With a limited stock of vehicles for sale in the UK, people have begun to source their dream vehicles abroad, where campervans can still be found at bargain prices. Large numbers are now being imported from Europe and the United States and RHD (right-hand-drive) models from Australia.

Until recently these countries were excellent sources of comparatively cheap campers in good condition, because Customs and Excise classed them as rare and/or historic vehicles, meaning that they carried only 5 per cent VAT. However, the importation into the UK of no fewer than 2,700 VW buses in 2004 alone led Customs and Excise to change the rules. No longer classed as rare or historic, imported campervans now carry 17.5 per cent duty (although there are some cynics who would say that the chance to increase revenue was the real motive for this change).

Even so, demand and interest continue to grow and prices continue to rise. A campervan is no longer a cheap and cheerful form of transport and the days of buying an old bus for a few hundred pounds are long gone. In 1990 rusty runabouts were the norm; nowadays it seems everyone wants a camper and the quality of vehicles seen at shows and used as daily drivers is quite stunning.

When we bought our Devon camper back in 1978 it cost £500 and we needed a loan to purchase her. In 2005 we spent over £12,000 restoring and refurbishing her; when we finally sold it in 2012 (to fund a new T5 California) it fetched £25,000! This dramatic surge in prices of old buses shows no sign of tailing off – a restored (or original condition) Split will now set you back around £30,000 and the highly sought after Samba models can cost £80,000 plus! Even the Bay window models command prices of around £15,000–20,000.

At these sorts of prices classic campers are now almost out of the reach of many families, and more and more people are turning to the T4 and T5 models. Most of these were former commercials or panel vans which have been transformed into stunning, fully equipped, bespoke campers. This growing trend is reflected in the numbers of these models at shows and they even have their own dedicated magazines. The T5 especially, which drives like a luxury car not a van, is bringing camping and a sense of freedom back to families.

Opposite: This 1954 Camper was painted as a psychedelic 'hippie' bus for an exhibition in the history of pop music (see page 83) in 2003.

9

EARLY DAYS

Interestingly, Volkswagen did not make any VW campers themselves until very recently. (In 2004, they finally launched their own plush version because their best-known maker, Westfalia, was by then owned by a rival motoring multinational conglomerate.) Instead, they licensed other companies to convert panel vans and Volkswagen Microbuses into campers. The most famous were those produced by the Westfalia Coachworks, but other names such as Devon, Dormobile, Danbury and Viking played an important part in creating affordable campers that opened up the UK market to the 'ordinary' person. South Africa, Australia and North America also had their own versions of the VW camper.

As affluence and leisure time increased through the 1950s, companies soon realised that there was a market for a vehicle that could serve simultaneously as a load-lugging workhorse, people-carrier and mobile holiday home. With its rugged reliability, high ground clearance, large interior space and easy-to-maintain air-cooled engine, the VW bus was ideal and was soon conquering the world.

Unbelievably, it all started with a crude, hand-drawn sketch. After the devastation of the Second World War, the massive reconstruction programme in Europe led to high demand for a basic delivery vehicle capable of carrying medium loads, and this was met initially by converting existing vehicles. The British Army was in charge of helping the German workforce to rebuild the Beetle factory at Wolfsburg and to get production running again. Ferdinand Porsche, the designer of the Beetle, came up with plans for a Beetle estate car/van but, although the idea found favour with the officer in charge of the factory, Major Ivan Hirst, production of the VW Beetle was considered to be the priority. In 1947 the Dutch motor dealer and importer Ben Pon visited the

Wolfsburg factory and saw a strange little factory-built flatbed, called a Plattenwagen, being used to transport parts around the factory. It was cobbled together from what was available and used a Beetle engine and running gear. He was so impressed by the potential of what he saw that he got his notebook out and drew a little sketch. Although somewhat crude, this sketch was the inspiration for what was to became the famous VW Transporter.

Below: Ben Pon's sketch, drawn in 1947, was the inspiration behind the birth of the VW Transporter.

Opposite top: The 4711 perfume company bought the first Transporter and painted it in the company livery in March 1950.

Opposite below: The Plattenwagen, used to ferry parts round the factory, gave Ben Pon the idea for what would become the VW Transporter.

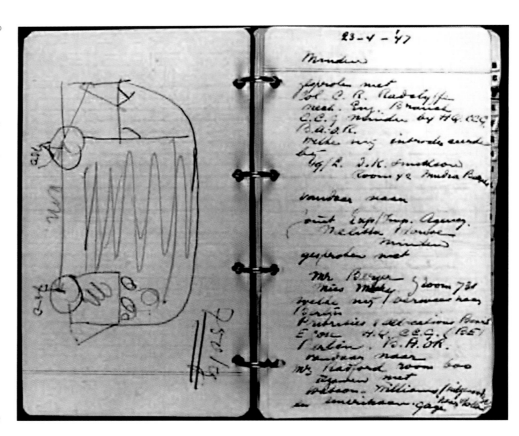

It had a box shape, an engine at the rear with opening hatch for access and a curved front with the driver positioned over the front wheels. Although the idea found favour, the factory was already fully stretched with limited resources and materials, and so the idea was shelved. However, in 1948 control of the factory was returned to the German people and Heinz Nordhoff was appointed as managing director. This visionary figure immediately saw the potential in such a vehicle and ordered the development of what was to become one of the most enduring icons of motor history. On 12th November 1949 the VW Transporter was presented to the world's press, in March 1950 it went into production and the rest is history.

Because the Transporter was originally conceived as a delivery van, the early vehicles were closed panel vans. Businesses were quick to see the potential offered for advertising, and the very first production-line vehicle was bought by the 4711 perfume company, which then immediately had it painted in its company colours, complete with logos.

From the Transporter's first conception, however, Nordhoff had had plans for a range of vehicles using the Transporter base, including a pickup truck and an ambulance. In May 1951 two new versions went into production – the Kombi, which had removable bench seating (with interior panels, insulation and a rear window as optional extras), and the nine-seater Microbus. In 1952 the Deluxe Microbus (known as a Samba in VW circles) was introduced, complete with sliding canvas roof, roof skylights, chrome fittings and high-level trim. All four models would later become bases for various camping conversions, with the Kombi the most popular base model for converters.

THE FIRST VW CAMPERS

In the early 1950s people simply could not afford a 'second' car, and therefore required a vehicle that could be used for work during the week but could double for family use at the weekend. The Kombi, with removable seating, met this demand perfectly.

The Martin Walter Company in the UK was among the first to see the potential of this newly expanding leisure market when, in 1951, one of the directors saw people sleeping in their cars at Dover while waiting for the ferry, and came up with the idea of a vehicle in which people could sleep in comfort. This became the Dormobile, one of the first of a new generation of affordable campers. The company was also among the first to put beds and cookers into vehicles, as well as developing the first elevating roofs. However, because VWs carried high import duties, Bedfords, Austins and Land Rovers were used for the early Dormobiles. It was a German company,

Westfalia, that would produce the first camping conversion on a VW base and set the standard for the future.

Westfalia was a long-established coachworks firm, known for the caravans and camping trailers it had produced in the 1920s and '30s. In 1951 an American officer serving in Germany asked Westfalia to design and build an interior for a VW Kombi styled on its caravan interiors. The company hand-built a further fifty fitted-out campers in 1951–52.

One of these hand-built, fitted-out prototypes was displayed at the Frankfurt Motor Show in 1952 and was bought by a couple of veteran travellers, Erna and Helmut Blenck, who travelled in it across South Africa in 1953. In 1955 they published a book about their travels in the camper, *South Africa Today: A Travel Book*, stating:

'For our previous trips to Asia, Africa and North America, we used an ordinary type car. This time, we were able to do what we had long planned: use a car that enabled us to cover great distances in comfort and stop for the night just when we wanted, quite independent of towns and hotels. But even more important than the possibility of sleeping in the car was the convenient way in which we were able to carry all our luggage. Today one easily forgets what a car, particularly its springs and tyres, has to stand up to on a trip like this, which took us at times over some very rough roads; the 14,000 miles that we covered in South Africa and South-West Africa must count double. We are very grateful for the way our Volkswagen Kombi and its Continental tyres carried us safely over all obstacles – sandy river beds, flooded roads, corrugations and exceptional gradients.'

Not only was the journey made by this first fitted-out VW camper, but it was also the first epic adventure undertaken by one and proved how well the vehicle could cope with rugged, inhospitable terrain. This camper and its journey demonstrated the capabilities of the little VW bus, which ever since then has been a favourite choice for travellers.

Knowing that the multi-purpose approach would be more popular and saleable than a permanently fitted camper, in 1953 Westfalia introduced the 'Camping Box' – a quickly installable and removable set of furniture that would enable a working van to be converted easily into a weekend camper. It consisted of seating for the side and rear and a large cabinet, fitted behind the front seats, that folded out to form a bed. There were also a simple cooker and washing facilities. The early brochures even showed how the furniture could be used at home to provide an extra bed for guests!

Demand was such, however, that in 1955 Westfalia reintroduced a fully fitted-out camper, available in Standard and Export versions. The next year, Peter Pitt, the founder of Canterbury Pitt Conversions, carried out the first VW camper conversion in the UK, and 1957 saw the entrance of Devon campers onto the scene. Things would never be the same again in the world of motorised caravans – the VW camper had arrived.

Right: The first Camping Box brochure was produced in 1953, extolling its multi-purpose uses.

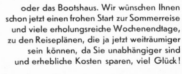

inraum, der im übrigen auch als Büro dienen
ihrend der Fahrt. Der Umbau zum Schlafraum
ichsene Personen finden so eine angenehme
wenn das Rückenpolster des Fahrersitzes waage-
bietet gleichzeitig einen sicheren Schutz
f der anderen Seite schützt die senkrecht
ns gestellt, bietet bequeme Sitzgelegenheit

Oben zeigen wir das große Zeltdach, das über die Galerie hinwegreicht und somit dem Wagen einen Wärmeschutz gibt. — In der Mitte sehen Sie das einfache Sonnensegel. Die bequeme Sitzbank (unteres Bild) die jetzt auch draußen zu verwenden ist, entsteht aus dem zusammenlegbaren Gestell mit Fahrer-Sitz- und Rückenpolster.

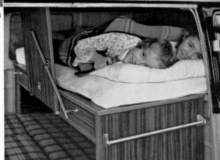

oder das Bootshaus. Wir wünschen Ihnen schon jetzt einen frohen Start zur Sommerreise und viele erholungsreiche Wochenendtage, zu den Reiseplänen, die ja jetzt weiträumiger sein können, da Sie unabhängiger sind und erhebliche Kosten sparen, viel Glück!

Haben wir nun zuviel gesagt, lieber Camping-Freund?
Ist die Vielseitigkeit unserer Wohneinrichtung „WESTFALIA-CAMPING-BOX" nicht wirklich verblüffend? Einfacher und bequemer geht es nicht, Ihrem rein gewerblichen Zwecken dienenden VW-Transporter eine neue Note zu geben. Doch nicht nur der Wagen allein macht nun mehr Freude. Nehmen wir an, Sie bekommen Besuch und Ihr Fremdenzimmer ist belegt, dann machen Sie es so, wie im obigen Bild, und auch dieses Problem ist gelöst. Die gleiche Möglichkeit bietet sich natürlich auch für die Jagdhütte

FIVE GENERATIONS

Many people think the designation Type 2 refers to the Bay Window campers, produced from 1967 to 1979. In fact, Type 2 is the generic name for all VW Transporters and buses, in the same way that all Beetles are Type 1.

There have been five generations of VW campers since the first VW Transporter rolled off the production line, but the best known are the Splitscreen (also known as the Split or Splitty) and Bay Window (often just called the Bay) versions. The Splitty gets its name from the distinctive divided front screen, making it instantly recognisable, and is thought by many to be the ultimate in cool. Often described as 'the van with a face' because of its V-shaped front panel, it definitely has retro appeal. There is a bit of snobbery in some circles of the VW camper world and, in the pecking order, the Split bus (bottom left), built between 1950 and 1967, reigns supreme. However, the Bay Window version (centre right), introduced in August 1967 with a distinctive one-piece curved front screen, is probably the best known version, and certainly the most common. Driving a Split is like stepping back in time to the days when things were simple and basic, while Bay Window campers are more comfortable to drive, have more power, handle better on the road and have brakes that work. Both models used the air-cooled engine with its distinctive putt-putt sound, and for many air-cooled campers are still the only campers worthy of any attention.

Production of the Bay ceased in 1979, when VW introduced the third generation of Transporter, known as the T3 or T25 (bottom right) in the UK and the Vanagon (from van and station wagon) in the United States and Canada. To some, these wedge-shaped campers are not 'real' VW campers. Although over the past few years they have been gaining in status and popularity, they don't have the cult following or appeal of the earlier versions. However, they are slowly becoming more accepted by the diehard air-cooled fraternity, and a glance round the camping fields at shows demonstrates just how popular they have become. Whereas a few years ago you could pick up a solid Split or Bay for a few thousand pounds, now you can expect to pay upwards of £20,000 for a reasonable Split and at least £12,000 for a sound Bay – and this has led to renewed interest in the T3; though cheaper, they too fetch more nowadays. In 1983 the air-cooled engine was consigned to history as being old-fashioned and outdated, and modern water-cooled engines were introduced – a sacrilege to many camper enthusiasts, who dismiss them as soulless water-pumpers and not real VWs. But times are changing and the T3 may, in time, achieve the cult status of the Splits and Bays. Although they may lack the charisma and character of the earlier campers, and on the outside are not so instantly recognisable, they are an important and integral part of the scene and their owners love them as much as any Split or Bay owner does.

In 1992 the T4 Transporter (centre left) was introduced. This looks like any modern box van and even has the engine at the front (horror of horrors). To reflect a changing market, these newer campers were very different affairs from their air-cooled predecessors, and the interiors used modern melamines and fabrics and were often better equipped and furnished than many homes, with microwaves, ovens, showers, satellite navigation and television, and CD/DVD-players as standard. However, while comfortable and well equipped, they lack the appeal of the old camper with its back-to-basics interior. Nevertheless, to have a heater that works, beds that do not need to be made up by laying out an intricate pattern of seat cushions, and a camper that does not require endless attention is a definite attraction. In fact, there are many camper owners who have both a modern camper and a classic camper and use them for different purposes, with their classic oldie remaining the lifestyle choice.

The T5, introduced in 2003, is the latest generation of VW Bus, and mainly marketed for commercial and MPV use. In the past VW had given prototypes of its new models to the Westfalia Werks in order for them to develop camper interiors to be ready for the introduction of the new models. However, with Westfalia now owned by Daimler/Chrysler/Mercedes-Benz group, VW was not about to give a rival the details of their new model T5 and it ended its special relationship with Westfalia in 2004, bringing fifty years of Westfalia campers to a close. However, Westfalia and VW renewed the relationship in 2013, launching a new generation of T5 Westfalia campers. Meanwhile, in 2004 VW produced the first ever factory built Volkswagen Camper called the California. Featuring an electrically operated aluminium elevating roof, faced aluminium cabinets and innovative design touches, such as camping chairs stored in the tailgate and a table in the sliding door panel, it is a world away from the simple basic campers of the past. The California (below) is currently the bestselling campervan on the market.

STOCK OR CUSTOM?

Another division in the classic VW campervan world is between the 'purists' and those who customise their camper. As in any hobby world, there are some who feel that original is best. They believe that everything should be kept 'stock' – ie, the camper should retain as many of its original features as possible – and they frown upon both 'lowered' buses and those painted in non-original colours. However, while lowering was once considered radical, it seems to have become the norm now. People like to dress their buses with special paint jobs, alloy wheels,

chrome accessories and individually chosen fabrics, from fake fur to Burberry.

A major part of the appeal of VW campers is the way owners can personalise them. Campers were made to be lived with, and one of the things that makes VW campers unique is this personal expression by owners who have created individual looks and characters for their vans. They are extensions of people's personalities and tastes, and this is an important part of their enduring appeal.

Stock buses are admired as pieces of living history, preserved for all to enjoy, while customised buses are individual expressions of creativity in a world of mass production and uniformity.

Two interesting trends have emerged in the past couple of years. The first involves the Performance Engine brigade, who keep their campers looking basically stock but who fit fast and powerful engines and enjoy racing them on drag strips. Seeing an old camper wheelie as the tyres screech and

smoke in the quest for a sub-14-second quarter-mile is quite something. These fast machines are all street legal, and the shock on a boy racer's face as his souped-up Fiesta GTi is left standing at traffic lights brings a smile to any face. Mind you, these modifications need radical changes to the old-fashioned braking system. Members of the recently formed BWA (Buses With Attitude) pride themselves on fitting performance engines to Split campers; to qualify for membership, a sub-18-second run over the quarter-mile is a requisite.

The second trend has become so widespread that there is now even a class for it at shows. A reaction against the vogue for shiny restored buses that are sometimes almost fashion statements, it is called the Rat Look. These buses are beaten and shabby, with faded paint and rust patches – the scabbier the paint, the better. The Rat Look is specifically cultivated by some owners, who have been known to bleach their paintwork or use sea water to achieve the desired effect, but for others it simply means no stress about scratches in shiny new paintwork!

Above: Typical 'Rat Look' bus.
Opposite top left: The 'Alien' has had a roof chop and body modifications, and has been lowered.
Opposite top right: Shorty is a cut-down Panel van.
Opposite below left: The huge engine lid is a feature of pre-1955 buses and the reason why they are nicknamed 'Barndoors'.
Opposite below centre: Stretched split camper.
Opposite below right: Campers on the drag strip.

CAMPERVAN CRAZY?

Whether stock or custom, vintage or modern, the appeal of the VW camper endures, and life with these funny little boxes on wheels is what this book is all about. Owners of VW campers are passionate about what they drive. While they may have different interests and tastes, they are all share one thing – an obsession with, and addiction to, the lifestyle of living with a VW camper. Whether chilling at shows with friends, holidaying with the family in France or brewing up in the Arctic Circle, owners are crazy about their campervans – and there are thousands of them out there. Are they crazy? Probably. But perhaps they know something others don't…

1 DESERTS, DOMES AND DREAMS

Unlike many, we stumbled into the world of the VW camper by chance (or was it fate?). We had spent most of 1975 planning and saving for an epic overland adventure. Inspired by a photo spread in *National Geographic* showing Renault 4 vans zipping about in the Bamiyan Valley and Hindu Kush, we had lined up a Renault 4 van for the journey. It seemed a good choice at the time. Then at the last minute the dealership decided to keep their works van, leaving us in the lurch. As we glanced through the ads in the local freebie news-sheet, the solution stared us in the face: '1967 VW campervan, tax, MOT, good condition, fast sale needed, £500.' It seemed too good to be true – a van already kitted out as a camper. We had no idea what a VW camper looked like, but the sight of two magpies crossing our path seemed a good omen as we set off to check it out.

As soon as we saw it outside the seller's house, we knew we had to have it. Everything was in good order, including the camping interior, and we left a deposit there and then. The seller explained that she was separated from her husband and needed a quick sale, so the first person to come up with the money could have it. We spent the next day frantically raising the cash, and returned to find she had the van ready for us and had even dumped all the stuff from inside onto the driveway. It was only later we found out the reason for the speed – she wanted it gone before her husband returned later that evening to claim it.

The camper was a Canterbury Pitt conversion, painted red and grey. We called her Momo after the main character in Michael Ende's novel *The Grey Gentlemen*. Momo fights the stealers of time who are turning people into a world of materialistic clones; somehow it seemed fitting. The equipment was fairly basic but it felt like luxury to us. The seating was arranged dinette style and the table dropped down between the two bench seats to form the bed. A small fold-down cooker (two burners and a grill) was mounted on the side door, and there was also a small sink with pump tap. A ten-gallon water container to feed this was sited under one of the bench seats. It was not long into the journey before we realised this tank was useless, as the stopper came off on bumpy roads and water slopped all over the place. Luckily we had brought five-gallon fresh water containers.

Everyone thought we were mad to give up secure jobs as teachers and head off to unheard-of places, but when you are in your mid-twenties, mortgages, children, pensions and jobs-for-life were things for the distant future. Life was for living now. Afghanistan, the Khyber Pass, Kashmir and the wild Hindu Kush lay out there somewhere! Our clock would be the sun; our daily plans would be decided as they unfolded. We had a route, places we hoped to see, but no time frame to guide us other than our own feelings.

We wanted to cross Europe as quickly as possible, before starting to take it day by day once Turkey had been reached. A detour to the Middle East had already been ruled out because of the instability of the region, so the plan was to follow the coast round the Mediterranean to the south, head up to Iran via eastern Turkey and thence to Afghanistan, Pakistan and India. The route was often referred to in those days as the 'hippie trail', but most of the people we met and journeyed with were, like us, ordinary people who wanted to do something extraordinary. The excitement came from never knowing what tomorrow would bring and being answerable only to ourselves. We might have been on a journey, but we were not on a quest!

For the first part of our journey we were carrying a friend, Sam. Though the campervan was only two-berth (it did not have an elevating roof), it did have a bench seat across the front cab, which made for a small third berth. However, after Sam had been rudely awakened on the second morning by a coach-load of female German pensioners peering through the front windows at his naked form, he opted to use his tent as often as possible.

Although we had had extensive repairs and servicing before we left home, there had been one problem that the garage could not fix – the reduction gears on the rear wheels needed attention and the garage had been unable to get parts. We stopped off in Frankfurt, hoping the VW garage there could help. Inside the workshops we found more than forty vehicle bays working flat out and mechanics who could not speak English (needless to say, we could not speak German). When we finally identified the problem for them by using workshop manuals, they fell about laughing. In halting English they advised us that it was far too expensive to fit and we should just go and buy another van! Eventually, though, they agreed to carry out the work, and the 'astronomical' bill, which would be more than the cost of a van in Germany, turned out to be around £200.

Previous pages, from left to right:
The Turquoise Coast, Turkey.
Carved stairway to the Great Hall of Darius, Persepolis, Iran.
A typical gravel road, Turkey.
The Kolahoi glacier, Kashmir.
The King's Mosque, Isfahan, Iran.

A doctor/patient consultation in Peshawar market. Note the live lizards, whose entrails were a remedy for vomiting.

The real start of the journey: Cee, Sam and Momo at the Austrian/Yugoslav border.

The Desert of Death, Afghanistan.

The road to Alanya fortress, Turkey. This is the moment the thermometer burst as it reached 140 degrees.

Kashmiri children in the mountain village where Momo was stored during our trek to the Kolohoi.

The European leg of the journey was drive and sleep. In Yugoslavia we began to notice the first signs that we were leaving Europe behind, and a hairy run-in with some rifle-waving army conscripts trying to commandeer a lift confirmed this. We had to make a long detour because a bridge had been partially destroyed by a rockfall. Many of the roads were gravel, none of the long tunnels were lit and the countryside was rugged and beautiful. It was beyond possibility that twenty years later this country would be ravaged by war and would give rise to the term 'ethnic cleansing'. So many of the ruins we were to see in our travels were the result of centuries of invasion, and it's sad to think that over the past thirty years so much of what was still intact then has now been lost for ever.

We had our first taste of the real benefits of the campervan when a tremendous thunderstorm hit one night. Having purchased some local wine at the roadside, we slept oblivious to the noise and chaos around us. The next morning, when we opened the doors, we were shocked to find the campsite awash, tents flattened and huddled groups of bedraggled people. Among them was our passenger Sam, who had been looking forward to a comfortable night stretched out in the privacy of his own tent.

From Yugoslavia, we dropped down into Greece, pausing long enough to rest by the sea and carry out a service on the camper. Then, once we had crossed the Bosphorus straits by ferry, we had left Europe, and the world we knew, firmly behind us.

Turkey was a bewildering mix of ancient and modern, of stunning scenery and archaeological treasures, of appalling roads and fearsome heat. It was in Turkey that we really began to appreciate what an excellent choice we had made in choosing a VW camper for the journey. We had been advised that the gravel-surfaced corrugated roads were best travelled at speed so that the tyres rode the bumps. Unfortunately, we never found that optimum speed, and everything just shook and rattled; it also created dust clouds that infiltrated every orifice, making visibility poor. That was my excuse for hitting a huge pothole anyway. There was a bone-jarring crunch, a sudden lurch, and for a moment we thought the van would not bottom out but just roll over. We pulled up, white-faced, to inspect the damage. The suspension and shock absorbers seemed all right, but the bumper mounting had come loose and caused some chassis damage. We limped off, only to find that the brakes were pulling violently to the right. Despite removing the hubs to inspect the drums and cylinders, we could find nothing obvious, and after a few miles it settled down to a less violent pull and we quickly learned to turn the wheel left when braking. (We never did manage to sort the problem out fully and had several scary moments when braking on mountain passes.)

One of the things we were to discover was that everyone seemed able to fix a VW. We stopped near Pamakkale and found the 'street of a thousand car-repair shops'. Choosing one at random, we negotiated a ridiculous price of around £5 to weld the bumper mount and repair the damage. It was only once work had actually started that we realised that the average age of the welders was around fifteen. We were reassured with friendly smiles and endless cups of chai, brought by a very small child. The work was completed within two hours – and never let us down, despite the hard roads we were to face. Leaving with more smiles and waves, we learned that the literal meaning of the farewell greeting gule gule was 'smiling smiling' – very apt.

The next thing we discovered was the reliability of the little air-cooled engine. Whatever the temperature, the camper just trundled on. On the coast near Alanya the dash-mounted alcohol thermometer reached 140°F and promptly burst. But air-cooled engines don't overheat, provided you treat them right and change the engine oil and dust filters regularly. We actually saw some travellers who thought that propping open the engine lid of their VW would allow more air in to keep the engine cool. However, the engine was designed to use a sealed compartment, and all that this did was drag in more dust and hot air, which would eventually lead to engine failure. We trusted the original designers and kept our lid firmly closed. It was hot. Dust got everywhere. We even resorted to travelling with moist hankies across our mouths, but still the dust found a way in.

Above: The Turkish mechanics who welded our road damage seemed to have an average age of fiftteen.

Opposite top: The Turquoise Coast of southern Turkey is aptly named.

Opposite below: The Cappadocian landscape looks like the setting for a surreal fantasy film.

On one long stretch of sandy desert, with the 'road' barely visible, the bus began to splutter. We were miles away from any village, let alone a town. We looked at the barren horizon then at each other. The engine coughed once more and died. With all that dust we reckoned that either the carb or the fuel pump must be choked. Fortunately, I had taken a car-maintenance course at night school before we left, and this was one thing I knew how to do. Not that I had actually done it before…

Apart from the heat there was one other small problem. I had stupidly drunk non-bottled water at a roadside chai-house and had developed severe stomach cramps and diarrhoea. (We later discovered it had been amoebic dysentery and very dangerous. It was fortunate that we had taken good advice about what to include in our medical kit, which even included anti-scorpion-bite serum.)

Anyway, I stripped the carb in the open sun, with a temperature of around 130°F, in between dashes to the other side of a sand dune. With carb and fuel pump cleaned and new filters in place, we turned the key and the bus started! Our joy was short-lived, though, as three miles up the road it died again with the same symptoms. Once again I cleaned everything in between bouts of dreadful stomach

Roadside crashes, like this one in Iran, were a familiar sight throughout the journey.

cramps. The bus started, and one mile up the road it died again. Then we realised the problem: it was so hot that the petrol was simply evaporating in the fuel lines or the carb. We wrapped them in wet tea towels, and bingo - the bus ran sweetly again, except that we had to keep stopping every few miles to moisten them. Even then we knew about engine-bay fires in VW campers.

We had found out the hard way about the road sign *Yol Yok* (literally 'the road is no more') but had no idea what *Yol Yapimi* meant – until we hit the roadworks. Most of the roads we travelled on were dust or gravel, but occasionally there would be a random stretch of tarmac. This tarmac surface was achieved by simply pouring liquid tar onto a smoothed section, and allowing it to set. Of course, in the extreme heat that took some time. We were still wondering what *Yol Yapimi* meant when we hit it: liquid tar all over the road. The vehicle spun and slid towards a steep drop. Cee applied the brakes and we spun the other way towards another drop. The bus rotated through two 180-degree arcs, each time veering towards an edge that would have meant doom. Everything seemed to go into slow motion and we really thought we would go over an edge, until finally the bus came to a halt. Tar was sprayed all over the back and sides. We were so relieved we burst into hysterical laughter and then put the adrenalin to use to clean her, using the fuel from Sam's spirit camping stove. We consoled ourselves with the thought that at least we'd never have to underseal the bus again.

The people in eastern Turkey were as inhospitable as the terrain we drove through. There were quite a few German travellers on the route, many of whom had fitted heavy-duty wire-mesh guards on every window. It was not long before we realised that all those German campervan drivers we had scoffed at knew something we did not. At the entrance and exit to every village, hordes of small boys armed with stones lay in wait. We soon learned how to deal with this, however: approach slowly, dangle an empty cigarette packet out of the window, slow down and throw it to them as we passed, then accelerate like hell while watching in the rear-view mirror as they

fought each other for the 'cigarettes'. By the time they realised the trick, we were a dust cloud. Mind you, we pitied the next group to pass that way.

The area around Lake Van was desolate and wildly beautiful. We stopped by the lake and discovered huge tortoises which not only moved fast but also had sharp teeth. Dislike of foreigners extended beyond the local wildlife: as the sun began to set over the lake, a truck drove by and fence posts and wood were hurled in our direction. Fortunately, the local police were passing and they came to our rescue, insisting we spend the night in the police station compound. They told us never to wild-camp, as bandits were operating in the area. The previous month a couple had been attacked and robbed, and the woman raped.

After an encounter with a bullock cart that had long, vicious knives attached to the wheels, Boudicca chariot style, we decided to head for Iran with all haste. It left an ugly scar down one side of the camper but we felt lucky to have come off so lightly. Our last memory of eastern Turkey was when Sam suddenly needed a toilet stop. We stopped near some rocks, miles from anywhere, and Sam disappeared while we started brewing up some tea. Suddenly there was the sound of loud barking and shouting. Looking up, we saw Sam running full pelt, clutching his trousers and closely pursued by three enormous dogs wearing collars on which were mounted huge spikes. He made it to the bus just before one of the dogs launched itself at the closing door. The dogs then laid siege, walking round and round Momo, growling and jumping up at the windows. Eventually we decided to leave the stuff we had outside the van and make a run for the border.

After waiting hours while our paperwork was checked at the border (the fastest we ever negotiated a border was five hours), we were into Iran and the relative luxury of tarmac roads. We had planned to stop at Tabriz, the first major town, but had not reckoned on the chaos caused by the Shah's visit to the area which brought everything to a total standstill. Even at that time it was clear that all was not well in this country, with locals being forced by armed police and soldiers to line the roads and cheer the passing cavalcade.

When we reached Tehran we decided to stop for much-needed repairs and a rest. The worldwide VW network meant that we got all the parts we needed from the local VW agent, whereas a couple travelling in a Land Rover had to wait six weeks for parts to arrive from England. Driving in Tehran was a total nightmare, with everyone seemingly in competition for who could drive the fastest or ignore the greatest number of red lights. Finding that the visas we needed for Afghanistan would take some time to arrange, we decided to head south and take in Isfahan. We also said goodbye at this point to Sam, who had a limited budget and time and thus decided to continue east by local bus.

Despite growing political unrest, the Iranian people were generally welcoming and friendly. As we drove south, all we could see was an endless black ribbon stretching into the distance, surrounded by every shade of beige and ochre. Sometimes huge, barren mountain ranges flanked the road, but mainly it was an endless vista of barrenness. Isfahan was an oasis of colour in the midst of all this, with green trees and dazzling domes of turquoise and mosaic dominating the town. Everything was clean and fresh. We camped in the grounds of a hotel and spent several days swapping stories with other travellers. On their recommendations we decided to head further south and visit the ruins of Persepolis, the capital city of ancient Persia.

Another long dusty drive through the endless landscape of rocks, sand and mountain ranges ended with one of the highlights of the trip. Walking around the ruins, fallen columns and intricately carved stones, one could not help but wonder at what had become of this rich civilisation and what skills had been lost along the way.

The nomad camp in southern Iran where the locals suddenly turned nasty.

Most roads in eastern Turky are gravel, dust and potholes.

We began to encounter groups of nomads tending camel herds and decided to stop to take some photographs. Immediately we were surrounded by brightly clad women and small children, who clustered around the van offering clothing, rugs, melons and tea. Unfortunately, one small boy caught his finger in the door jamb and began to wail hideously. In an instant the mood turned ugly and we could see men armed with sticks heading out of the tents. One old woman (obviously the matriarch) began to mobilise the crowd and hit the van with her stick. We shut the windows, hit the gas pedal and churned up a cloud of dust and gravel as stones and sticks were thrown after us.

Resolving to steer well clear of nomad camps from then on, we headed back to Tehran to pick up our visas and decided to make for Afghanistan by way of the Caspian Sea and Meshed. There was a more direct route to the east, but this involved rough tracks crossing a desert, with no petrol stations for 300 miles. Despite carrying jerrycans for just such a scenario, we did not fancy it, and opted for the longer tarmac route. At the Caspian Sea we turned east once more and settled back into a routine of driving towards the rising sun. It was at this point that we suffered our first and only puncture, but with two spare wheels on the roof rack specially made by the design department at my previous school, it was not a problem. Meshed was full of pilgrims and rip-off merchants offering 'bargain' carpets and turquoise jewellery. Naïvely we didn't realise that 'free tours' around carpet and jewellery workshops ended with high-pressure sales, and we counted ourselves lucky to have only had to buy some gemstones to set later.

And then we were in Afghanistan. Of all the places we travelled around, Afghanistan was the jewel in the crown. We still feel privileged to have been introduced to the culture, customs, peoples and landscapes of this proud and wild land, much of which has now been destroyed. So many of the places we travelled peacefully through in 1976 were to change dramatically for ever.

As soon as we entered Afghanistan it felt like time had stopped. We had gradually lost a sense of time on the journey, but we were travel-weary, and when we arrived in Herat just across the border we quickly settled into a routine of rest and relaxation. Days were spent ambling round the streets and markets of the old town, exploring the city walls and ruins, sitting in tea houses watching the world go by or chatting under shady vines in the gardens of the Friends Hotel. The hotel's resident pelican provided hours of amusement, especially as he was partial to stealing anything he could fit in his beak. We luxuriated in the fact that a shower was available, until we discovered that the tank was topped up each morning using water from the pelican's pond! A one-legged, one-armed cigarette salesman visited everyday in his wheelchair – and each day we haggled the price down. We wondered if we would ever have reached a point where he would have given them to us for nothing.

The couple we had met in Tehran, waiting for parts for their Land Rover, rolled in and decided to take the vehicle up into the mountains – they limped back two days later with a broken drive shaft, while a VW bus that had hooked up with them for the excursion came back intact. Another VW camper arrived, having travelled the northern route via Mazar-i-Sharif. The mountain roads had been so atrocious that the bus had gone over the edge at one point, rolling through several sideways-on somersaults in the process. Amazingly, no one had been hurt, and a local lorry and lots of villagers had managed to pull the bus back up onto the road.

The body and roof looked like corrugated cardboard but the drivers were confident they could make it back to Europe. Travellers came and went, but we were blissfully happy just to savour sitting in one place after so long on the road – until we suddenly realised that we had been in Herat for two full weeks and now had only two weeks left on our visa.

To reach Kabul we had to loop a long way south to Kandahar. Even before seeing the fate of the bus that had taken the shorter, northern loop, we had already decided that it was just too much for us to handle. The Russian-built tarmac road cut a direct swathe through the unrelenting terrain of mountains, desert and scrub. Mud-built villages merged with the landscape, the heat haze made the black snake that stretched ahead of us shimmer and move like a living creature, and people carried out their lives in a way unchanged for centuries.

In one mountain pass we met a French couple travelling by bicycle. When I remarked how brave they were, the response was a philosophical 'Zometimes you haz to be brave!' We, however, were glad to have the security blanket of our trusty little camper. We had been warned about the effects of high altitude on engine performance but we never experienced any of them. The Afghan petrol was low-grade, 70 octane stuff – which played havoc with the engines of the two Bay Window buses we were now convoying with to Kabul, causing them to splutter and 'pink' – but Momo took it all in her stride.

Our sojourn in Kandahar was memorable only for a severe bout of dysentery for Cee and queuing for hours to change money. Cee was too poorly to travel but our new friends decided to stay put with us, despite the fact that they, too, were running out of visa time. Eventually we headed up to Kabul, this time on an equally good road built by the Americans.

Flash floods were obviously a common occurrence because when the road hit a wadi (a ravine that is dry except in the rainy season), it simply stopped; a loose track, usually littered with boulders, crossed the wadi, and the tarmac restarted on the other side. As we neared Kabul, traffic began to increase – nomad camel trains and bullock carts fought brightly painted lorries and minibuses for road space. We had to thread our way very gingerly indeed.

Kabul has always been the crossroads for travellers in the Hindu Kush, and its streets were thronged with colour, noise and humanity. We found an excellent camping area in the grounds of a hotel right in the heart of the city, and I set off to buy something for Cee's recovering stomach. To my surprise the shops sold everything imaginable – I returned with a tin of Campbell's chicken soup for Cee and a huge piece of lemon meringue pie for myself. We never felt unsafe in Kabul, though we did give dogs a wide berth, having heard travellers' tales of rabies. The chador was much in evidence – frequently Cee would suddenly find herself being addressed in perfect English by women completely covered apart from their eyes. They were fascinated by all things western – a strange paradox.

We enquired about the road to Bamiyan and Band-i-Amir and decided it would be better to travel by local bus – and we were very glad we did. The minibus bumped and climbed its tortuous way (sometimes with no sign of the actual road), stopping every few miles to pick up villagers. At one point there were ten people and two goats travelling on the roof. Every hour, everything stopped for fifteen minutes of prayer. Finally, after eight hard hours' travel, the walls closed in and we negotiated a gorge just eight feet wide. When the rock faces on either side finally parted, there in front of us lay the fertile and spectacular Bamiyan Valley, dominated by

two huge statues of the Buddha carved directly into the cliff face.

Some of the most serene moments of my life were spent watching the sun rise and set over the Buddhas. As the sun rose you could literally see the darkness fall away in front of you as the sun breathed life and colour into the world, gradually moving up the cliff face to cloak the shadowy statues in energy, giving them form and substance. I felt connected in time through centuries, and though the statues had been defaced (literally) by Islam centuries before, they had lost none of their awesome beauty. In a strange way, having no faces made them even more mysterious and powerful.

The Buddhas of Bamiyan no longer exist. Religious fervour had removed their faces; religious fanaticism destroyed them. The Taliban fired salvo after salvo of rockets into the cliff face, and one of the wonders of the ancient world is now lost to us for ever. But as Buddha himself said, all is impermanence. All things pass. But my memories endure.

We had heard of the fabled lakes of Band-i-Amir, but nothing could have prepared us for the surreal tapestry of lakes and mountains laid before us. Set in the heart of the Hindu Kush at an altitude of 8,800 feet, the lakes looked like beads of lapis lazuli set in a Dali-esque landscape. It was here a local tribesman said to us, 'I don't know why you tourist peoples are so frightened of us. We only kill two or three of you a year.' The scary thing was that he was not joking. We arrived back in Kabul feeling humble and insignificant. The camper was by now due for another service and we had to leave for the Khyber Pass and the border before our visa expired in three days' time. So when someone came round all the VWs parked in the grounds offering to do servicing at his new premises in the next street, it sounded too

good to be true – and it was. The inspection pit consisted of ramps made of two long mounds of earth with a hole dug between them, and the mechanic must have been all of sixteen years old. I supervised his work with a stony face, but when he started pulling on the flexible brake hoses to remove them, I snapped before the brake hoses did. We carried out the service ourselves back at camp. Amazingly, there was even a VW dealership in Kabul – they fitted new shock absorbers and a battery (which they sourced in the bazaar) to our friends' bus and carried out some much-needed welding to their battery tray, which was about to fall through the chassis at any moment.

We also needed to top up our gas cylinder and called in at a local Calor gas shop. They willingly filled our bottle for a few pence. The trouble was, they didn't weigh the bottle to see when capacity was reached – they just filled it till no more would go in, at which point gas started hissing out through the valve. Considering that the gas cylinder in the camper was sited in the engine bay, this was a bit scary. We left it hissing for a whole day, before resorting to releasing gas by poking a screwdriver in the valve.

The Khyber Pass was as wild as it looks in films. Jeeps carrying bearded tribesmen, with rifles and ammunition belts slung across their shoulders, honked as they overtook dangerously on blind bends. Hairpin after hairpin clung to the side of the mountain and we half-expected to see a British column of red-coated soldiers appear at any moment.

In Peshawar we found a dak bungalow (a traveller's rest-house) but were a little perturbed when we were allocated armed guards (who looked scarier than bandits). Apparently there was a local blood feud and they wanted to ensure we did not get caught up in crossfire. We left at first light the next day!

Resident pelican and cigarette salesman in the hotel grounds. Herat.

The first sight of Band-i-Amir looks more like a painting.

Natural dams form the lakes of Band-i-Amir.

High up in the Hindu Kush the temperatures are very cold.

Afghan and Pakistani lorries were works of art, decorated with religious and good luck symbols.

The road into the mountains around Lake Dal, Kashmir.

Houseboats on Lake Dal, Kashmir.

The large Buddha of Bamiyan. Unfortunately both Buddhas were destroyed by the Taliban.

Typical scene on the side of the Grand Trunk Road, India.

With winter closing in the trek back was a race against snow and storms.

After the empty wildernesses we had travelled through, Pakistan assaulted the senses, with a mass of humanity at work or on the move. Streets seethed with cows, bullock carts, donkeys, rickshaws, colour, noise and people. Never had we seen so many people. Everywhere we went they wanted to talk to us or simply stare at us. We would pull up for a loo stop, or a brew, in what seemed deserted countryside, and within minutes people would appear as if by magic and crowd round us. Favourite questions were the current state of Elizabeth Taylor's love life (they assumed we must know her personally as we were English) and whether we had met a cousin/brother/ uncle who lived in London/Birmingham/Bradford. It was about this time that Momo developed her only other problem of the entire journey – a sticky starter solenoid switch, meaning you would turn the ignition key and just hear a loud 'clunk'. Luckily there were always hordes of willing volunteers ready to push-start her.

The roads were lined with vendors selling anything and everything. Cee spotted one selling what looked like nightlights, so we pulled up. However, when we approached, the stall holder flicked a towel over the 'nightlights' and the 'wicks' flew into the air in a black cloud – what we had seen were chunks of round sugar cane covered with flies.

We finally crawled to the border to find that India had declared a state of emergency. The officials were jumpy about letting anyone cross, but a wad of rupees folded inside a passport saw us on our way in just a few hours. We had reached India at last.

Driving on the Grand Trunk Road was another new experience. It was tarmac, but potholed and only just wider than a lorry. The only way to drive it was to hug the middle of the road and play chicken with any oncoming lorry or bus – if you pulled to one side too early the lorry would simply stay in the middle and force you off the road. The aim was for both vehicles to give way at the final moment, so that only one set of wheels drove through the rough gravel at the roadside. What was more, the people seemed unaware of vehicles – we wished that we had a huge air horn. By the time we turned north for Kashmir we were feeling somewhat travel-worn, but the road ahead was to be the hardest we had faced so far.

The road into Kashmir winds for 150 miles through gorges, valleys and mountain passes, rapidly rising and falling through countless hairpins. At times it clings precariously to the side of a mountain with steep drops to a river below, while at others it undulates through valley floors with terraces of rice fields climbing away on either side. In many places it is only wide enough for one vehicle, and twisted wreckage littering the roadside is testament to how dangerous this road is to drive. On a number of occasions we were held up while gangs of villagers, the women carrying rocks for the men to break, were engaged in repairs where the road had simply slipped away. Fortunately (?) the fact that the military needed to use the road meant it was kept open, although there were times when we had to stop and wait for convoys of up to fifty trucks of soldiers and equipment. After two days of tortuous bumping and stressful driving, we finally reached the highest point and entered a single-track tunnel.

The sight that greeted us when we emerged from that tunnel is indelibly etched on our memories. Spread below was a vast valley of green, completely encircled by massive snow-capped peaks marching into the distance in every direction. The sun was just setting, tingeing the distant mountain tops with pink and gold against a deepening azure sky – it was literally breathtaking.

When we arrived in the capital, Srinagar (which, no matter how we tried, we could never pronounce as the locals did), we found that because of political instability farther north, Leh ('Little Tibet') and Ladakh were closed to foreigners. This also explained the heavy military build-up clogging the only road in. Fortunately, before we had left we had arranged to stay on one of the many houseboats on Lake Dal. Although our arrival date had not been specified, Mr Razak welcomed us with open arms and made us feel special. It was now late autumn and the tourist season was slack, so we had discounted rates. The houseboat was a five-star affair, complete with our own cook (ex-Indian Army) and 'houseboat boy'.

After many weeks on the road, it was time to do nothing except watch the world go by and the sun rise and set over the mountains. We shopped in bazaars for trinkets and carved boxes; we chatted in chai houses; we ate like kings. The influence of the days of the Raj was still evident and we lived the life of the idle rich, while trying to reconcile our comfortable existence with the grindingly hard lives of those all round us.

Mr Razak offered us the chance to trek on horseback up into the surrounding mountains to the Kolahoi glacier; it was only when we arrived in Momo at a village that we realised we were expected to leave our precious home there. Initially we may have offended the village elders by showing concern about leaving Momo with them, but they produced tarpaulins and two armed 'guards' and assured us it was their privilege to care for our home – and what alternative was there? We took a leap of faith, and on our return were presented with a gleaming Momo that had just been washed.

The other thing we had not really understood was the reality of trekking on horseback, when neither of

us had ever been on a horse before. Fortunately, our mounts were small mountain ponies rather than horses, and they were extremely sure-footed. This was just as well, as the track was even more scary than the road in – so much so that on several sections I opted to walk.

From the base camp at an altitude of 11,500 feet we were able to walk and ride deep into the heart of the mountains, and get close up to the stunning Kolahoi peak and glacier. On the third day we were heading for a small lake which involved crossing several mountain passes when it began to get really cold. Our guides kept looking at the sky and muttering to each other. It soon became apparent that the weather was turning, and eventually they told us we would have to turn back. We rapidly retraced our steps as visibility lessened and the clouds closed in around us, until eventually we had to be roped together. We managed to return to base just as the rain began. That night a thunder and lightning storm raged all round us, while we huddled in sleeping bags feeling the earth tremble. We awoke next morning to find brilliant sunshine and two feet of snow hemming us in – and no horses! They had bolted in the thunderstorm and it took the guides nearly four hours to find them. Winter had arrived, and we had to get back down the mountain while we still could. We knew it was serious by the way the guides kept hastening us along, their smiles and jokes replaced by frowns and constant glances at the skies, which were again darkening rapidly. When we made it back to the village we were told that the route we had just travelled would now be virtually impassable until the spring.

Arriving back at the houseboat we realised that unless we headed off soon, we were likely to be snowed in for the whole winter. Although the Indian Army would try to keep the road open, the thought of negotiating that twisty route back through snow and ice was too much even to contemplate. And while Kashmir was timeless and serenely beautiful, it was time to move on. We bade fond farewells, serviced Momo ourselves and were back on the road again.

We toured northern Punjab, marvelling at the Golden Temple in Amritsar, before taking the Grand Trunk Road to Delhi. By now we were again feeling overwhelmed by the teeming mass of humanity, the terrible poverty and squalor, the children disfigured by parents so that they could more easily beg, the stench. India was beautiful and terrible at the same time. We loved it; we were fascinated by it; we were humbled by it – but we longed for wild, open spaces once more. Christmas was approaching fast, and as our thoughts began to turn to friends and family at home, we had a difficult decision to make: whether to return to England before winter set in and made travel nigh on impossible in certain places (including eastern Turkey), or to head deeper into India and start our return the following spring. We decided it was time to head back.

Travelling out had been a leisurely affair, with no sense of urgency. We had lived each day as it came, time was irrelevant and our body clocks were tuned to the pace of the earth. The journey back would prove to be very different, as we were racing the onset of winter. Previously we had sometimes travelled only fifty miles in a day – now we would have to average 400 miles a day to try to get across the Hindu Kush, Iran and eastern Turkey before it became almost impossible.

Border crossings became frantic affairs. At the Afghan border we were made to unload everything onto a dusty courtyard. The officials poked and prodded everywhere, prised off Momo's panels and let down her tyres. When we tried to plead, we were met with shrugs and comments like, 'I don't care whether I let one car or ten through here in a day. Got any whisky or dollars or *Playboy* magazines?' None of which we had. Finally a bribe of a foot pump and some cassette tapes obtained the right stamps on the right bits of paper, and we literally threw everything back into the bus and fled.

When we reached the Iranian side, the process started all over again – though at least this time there were metal benches on which to stand everything. Trained by the CIA, the Iranian officials knew their business and were very methodical. They even held a hand on our hearts while questioning us to see if our blood pressure was racing. They were confused by our liquid OXO (beef extract) in a dispenser bottle and were convinced the black gooey substance must be hash oil. They kept tasting and sniffing it until Cee made them a hot drink from it, whereupon they actually smiled.

An American couple we were now travelling with were not so lucky. They had argued with the Afghan border officials and shouted at them. Big mistake – we had learned early on that pointing a finger and shouting were a sure-fire ways to ensure total non cooperation from any official. The customs officials set about completely stripping out everything from their Mercedes camper, including all the panelling for the on-board shower. When they finally limped through to Iran the next day and saw us repacking the van surrounded by smartly dressed officials and armed police, they wisely kept quiet!

On the way out, Momo had coped with extreme heat; on the return she was subjected to extreme cold. The butane gas froze (luckily we had propane as a back-up) and water would freeze the instant it was poured into a container. We slept in our clothes inside sleeping bags, and still shivered. Lorry drivers would light fires under their vehicles each morning to thaw the diesel, and a Commer camper we travelled with for a while cracked its cylinder block because the antifreeze could not cope. Of course, we had none of that trouble – the air-cooled VW camper could cope with any extreme of temperature, though the crude heating system never kicked in as the outside air was so cold. We drove virtually non-stop from dawn to dusk with hot-water bottles and blankets on our laps, scraping ice from inside the windscreen and chain-smoking to calm our nerves and keep our fingers warm!

We entered eastern Turkey the day after one of the biggest earthquakes ever seen in that region. To add to the chaos, the temperature was minus 15°F, coating everything in ice. Petrol was virtually unobtainable, and when we did find some it had to be hand-cranked as all power in the region was out.

Having an Afghan stamp in our passports was a bit like having the dreaded Black Spot – at every border post on the way home the officials would look through the passport, see that stamp and order us to strip everything out of the van. Greece was cold and snowy and Yugoslavia a nightmare of fog, snow and ice. We stopped to tow a stranded VW and promptly got fined for driving too slowly on the autoput (highway). At the German border we said we had just come from Greece (sort of true) but one look at the Afghan stamp and it was everything out of the van again. They spent a long time deciding whether to let us in as we had no snow chains on the tyres. After we had crossed the border we soon found out why, as even the autobahn across the Alps was blocked for several hours.

Twenty miles from the Channel ferry we ran into one of the most torrential hailstorms we had ever experienced. The storm followed us as we crossed the Channel and the bar was as empty as most people's stomachs. When we finally began to disembark, the exit slipway was rising and falling alarmingly in front of us. Surprisingly, UK customs were not really interested in us. Even though we tried to show them everything we had bought, in case we had to pay duty, they waved us through. Momo had carried and cared for us for 27,000 miles; our home was back home.

Six months later we had to sell her to raise money for a deposit on a house. But travel and the VW camper were now embedded in our psyches. It took two years to save for a replacement, and when we picked up Momo 2, the seller's children were drawing pictures of their beloved camper and crying. That was in 1978. Since then Momo 2 has taken our three children and ourselves all over Europe, and now there is a grandchild waiting to holiday in her. We can't imagine life without our campervan, and while we enjoy the lively VW bus scene and shows, the lifestyle of going where we want, and stopping when we please, is still fundamentally what it is all about.

The authors by the lakes of Band-i-Amir. At an
altitude of nearly 9,000 feet the air is thin, but
as crystal clear as the lakes.

While some stumble into the VW camper world, and others make a conscious lifestyle choice, there is also a hard core of camper owners who grew up with a VW camper, went on family holidays in one and now have their own campers. It's almost as if there were a VW camper gene passed down the generations, or, as some would say, 'It's in the blood.' Nature or nurture? Or both?

FROM VINTAGE BEETLE

Simon Holloway's story is a classic example of someone whose early influences and memories are of VWs. However, while many VW babies grow up and return to the campervan fold as second- or third-generation bus owners, Simon has gone one step further, to become one of the most influential people in the VW camper scene. Without Simon's driving force and passion there would be no Type 2 Owners Club and no Vanfest. Vanfest was born from Simon's vision of creating the biggest VW bus festival in the world, and the event is now almost legendary within VW bus circles and a must-get-to show for all campervan owners.

The story starts with Simon's father's 1947 Beetle, which came back with him to the UK from Germany in 1957. This had been a British Control Commission vehicle and one of the first Beetles to roll off the newly rebuilt production line at Wolfsburg. Like all early VWs, it was 6-volt with a crash gearbox (no synchromesh in those days!). Simon was conceived on the back seat of this vehicle, which may explain why VWs are in his blood.

Around 1961 the family moved to Aden (now South Yemen) but they could not be without a VW and soon acquired a 1954 ragtop (canvas-sunroof) Beetle. They quickly learned the local trick of covering the paintwork in coconut oil to prevent it from burning off and blistering in the sun. Simon, then aged five, used to drive the Beetle along the endless Arabian

beaches. As he was too small to see over the windscreen, he would stand on the seat and peer out of the open roof. In 1962 the family moved once again, this time to Kenya where they acquired yet another VW Beetle.

On their return to the UK in 1963, the family moved from Beetles to campervans, the ideal solution for a growing VW-obsessive family. Simon went with his dad to pick up the latest family member from a garage in Reading – a brand-new red and white Splitscreen camper, which was the latest model from the newly merged company Canterbury Pitt. Having christened the camper Victoria, the family had many happy holidays with it in the UK and loved it so much that when they moved to Malta in the late 1960s, the van went with them.

In 1969 the family moved yet again, this time to Singapore. Simon's father's first attempt to buy a VW fell foul of a language misunderstanding – he ordered a VW Variant from a Chinese dealership and was told it was 'no ploblem'. However, two weeks later when he went to pick it up, he

found that they had mistakenly ordered him a Valiant – a huge Canadian thing complete with fins, which, to the family's embarrassment, he decided to keep until he could find a VW.

It was not long before the family had another camper, this time a 1964 Kombi, which had originally started life as a CKD (Completely Knocked Down) kit assembled in Australia. The bus had already made an overland journey from Australia to the UK and back to Singapore, but despite being well travelled it was still in excellent order. Known affectionately as Matilda (because it waltzed down the roads), this camper took the family, which now numbered five, all over Malaysia. Its humble 1200cc engine never once let them down, even on the most primitive of roads. They travelled extensively in some very out-of-the-way areas, and Simon has vivid memories of waking up on remote beaches to find hordes of local inhabitants gathered round the camper to see the white people in the strange vehicle. He also remembers that the awning was a primitive contraption, stored on the full-length roof rack; for camping, the supports and poles that were fixed in place on the rack were swung out ready for the canvas to be pulled over them – very sturdy and quick to erect.

The family returned to the UK in 1971, and getting another camper was the first item on the agenda – this time a 1968 Devon Bay, called Bluebell because of its colour. It stayed with the family for the next twenty-five years, moving with them back to Germany and then finally on to New Zealand.

Previous pages, from left to right:

The good thing about a camper is its versatility - how else do you transport your personal flying machine?
A family camper at a family wedding, snapped in 1960.
Over 3,000 campervans now make the annual pilgrimage to Vanfest every September.
Modern colours for a new generation of owners.
Camping in Malaysia in 1969.

The 1947 Beetle at Portpatrick railway station, Galloway, Scotland (one of Simon's father's first postings on their return to the UK in 1957). The coach-built pram contains the infant Simon. His mother is in the doorway of the caravan that was their home before they moved into the disused station building.

TO VANFEST

The Holloways' 1954 sliding-roof Beetle, pictured near Ras Imran in 1962. It used the local remedy of being covered with coconut oil to stop its paint from blistering off in the heat of the southern Arabian Desert.

The Holloways' first camper, bought new in 1963, was one of the new Canterbury Pitt models.

'Matilda' leaving Singapore en route for the UK via Burma, India and the Khyber Pass, crewed by one male and three female Kiwis. The camper turned up to see the family some three months later when they arrived in the UK, but shortly after that it was sadly written off in an accident on the M4 motorway.

Camping in Malaysia in 1969.

Simon with his mother, sister and surrogate family member, on the Ngong Hills track near Nairobi in 1962.

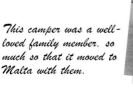

This camper was a well-loved family member, so much so that it moved to Malta with them.

'Bluebell' at a campsite in Littlehaven, Pembrokeshire, circa 1974.

Simon 'officially' learned to drive in Bluebell (as well as other things a teenage lad would find a camper useful for!). All the Holloway children were attached to her, and, like a family heirloom, the camper was passed down through the three children before it was finally sold to a young Kiwi family. Now completely restored, it is still going strong down under.

Simon subsequently met and married Audrey. Problems with the purchase of a new family home led them to buy a ropey Devon camper to act as temporary home, but a few weeks actually turned into several months.

With VWs and campers embedded in his life, it is no surprise that Simon became active in the club scene, ending up as coordinator for the 'Bug-In' event (later

to become BVF). At Bug-In '90, he introduced and presented the first Special Display, which, like Show & Shine or Concours events, was to become a regular feature of most VW shows throughout the country. As Bug-In '90 was the fortieth anniversary of the VW bus, the obvious choice for the Special Event was a Type 2 exhibition. Simon had joined the Splitscreen Van Club because of its family and social side, and it became clear from the response and enthusiasm this display generated that there was a need for a similar club catering for owners of post-1967 buses. This gave Simon the impetus to set about forming a new club for owners of these buses – and, with the support of a few other dedicated individuals, the Type 2 Owners Club was born.

One of the things the club initially hoped to do, as well as providing friendship and support for like-minded owners of VW campers, was to set up a show dedicated exclusively to VW buses. This led to the establishment of the ultimate event for VW camper and bus lovers, Vanfest, held every September at the foot of the stunning Malvern Hills in Worcestershire. The event now draws over 3,000 campervans and 18,000 people, all of whom are there to enjoy and celebrate living with a VW camper. As soon as one Vanfest finishes, Simon and his dedicated team are busy planning the next.

Simon currently owns two rare VW buses. The T25 Syncro has 4WD off-roading capabilities to make a Land Rover weep, while the long-wheelbase Kemperink is a Dutch-built conversion of which very few survive. (Simon's seventeen-year-old son Lloyd, who has obviously inherited the VW gene, has already set his sights on this one.)

Top: The Dutch-converted Kemperink was originally a bread van before being kitted out as a camper.

Above: Simon's daily driver is a T25 Syncro, with off-road capabilities.

CHILDHOOD MEMORIES

Family camping, 1950s-style.

Miles Newman's family owned what must have been one of the first RHD buses imported into the UK – a 1954/5 'Barndoor' Kombi, with removable bench seating. Although it was not kitted out as a camper, the family used it as one by removing the middle seats. The parents slept on an airbed on the floor, while one child slept on the front bench and the other over the engine compartment. In the late 1950s the family regularly went on holidays to Wales and Scotland, with the bus's interior packed with camping equipment. One of Miles's earliest

memories is of waking up in the camper on a deserted Welsh beach, peering around the curtain and seeing a baby rabbit running across the sand dunes. He drew pictures of the rabbit in the overnight condensation on the unlined roof as the drips fell onto his ex-army sleeping bag. Miles still carries a permanent reminder of his campervan childhood in the form of a scar inside his bottom lip, the result of colliding with the windscreen while sitting on his mother's lap when his father suddenly braked hard. He also fondly remembers his dad

discovering clutchless gear-changing after he accidentally depressed the floor-mounted dipswitch instead of the clutch; having got the revs right anyway, he sailed smoothly into the next gear with ill-suppressed chuckles.

About four years later the family progressed to a green and white Devon Caravette. After the spartan interior of the Kombi, the Devon was considered luxurious, with a lined roof (no more condensation drips), proper beds, interior gas lighting and a cooker.

Winter camping in the Cairngorms.

Summer holiday in the Alps.

What stands out most in his mind, however, was the distinctive smell, which, with hindsight, he thinks was probably leaking gas! The most memorable experience of living with that camper was in 1965, when the family was returning from a day's conservation work and had to negotiate a deeply flooded main road near Slimbridge, where the River Severn had burst its banks. After they had manoeuvred carefully around several abandoned cars, a lorry coming towards them pushed a bow-wave so high that when it hit the front of the Caravette the wave kept on going, right over the top. Luckily the engine just kept chugging away.

Miles cites *Alice's Restaurant* as a movie that touched his psyche in 1970. His early memories of living in a VW camper, not to mention a converted Congregational chapel, gave the movie a special resonance for him. Despite this, it would be thirty years before Miles got his own VW camper, an impressive T25 Leisuredrive conversion. Now he is back reliving the freewheeling spirit of his childhood and, with his wife Jo, travelling and camping as often as they can – whether battling blizzards in wintry Scotland or soaking up the summer sun in Italy. Even though the camper has all the basic creature comforts, Miles says, 'Our VW T25 is undoubtedly the best van in the world, but I do still sometimes wonder why we might think we need anything more than a panel van, an awning, an airbed, a washing-up bowl and a primus stove.'

LIKE FATHER, LIKE SON

The camper was the perfect vehicle for the new style of family holidays of the 1960s, and the Ward family were typical campervan owners of the time. They bought their first Devon in 1963, only replacing it in 1966 for the new Devon model, which featured VW refinements such as 12-volt electrics. Throughout this time the family enjoyed holidays together, often in Wales and Scotland.

When the new generation Bay Window models came out in August 1967, Allan (then aged eighteen) pestered his father, Ray, to update the Splitty camper for this latest model, emphasising its speed, road-holding and all-round improvements, such as IRS (Independent Rear Suspension). It was no easy task, especially as Ray saw no reason to change something reliable he had grown to love. Raymond Ward was not the kind of person to rush into anything, and he carefully checked out the competition from Danbury and Dormobile. But nothing came close to the style, luxury and layout of the top-of-the-range new Devon Eurovette. It even came with an oven as standard! They ordered it in October 1967, but it was March 1968 before the family took possession of their third brand-new VW Devon camper. The cost of £1,331 was offset by a part-exchange deal of £950 for the 1966 camper. This sold so quickly that when Ray went to collect his new Devon there was someone waiting on the forecourt to take delivery of his '66.

Over the next couple of years Ray had the dealership install a range of extras and features, including black pin-striping round the waistline, a rear screen heater, a radio and a battery-charging unit that simply plugged into the mains, allowing the battery to be charged in situ. Also fitted were reversing lights, rear fog lights, front spot and fog lights and a badge bar for the RAC and AA metal badges, and he moved the spare wheel from its plastic holder to the front. Apparently all this was Ray's way of protecting the front from stone chips. Back in 1974 ICE was a choice between Eight-Track and the new car cassette players (a bit like the Betamax and VHS video war – no one knew which would win out). Luckily Ray opted to fit the new-style car cassette player, and the camper still sports this working example of a very rare period accessory. Another interesting accessory is a dash-mounted compass, which is electrically powered and lights up when the headlights are on.

Ray was fanatical about keeping 'the Volkswagen', as the camper was known, pristine – it never went out in the rain and if there was an unexpected shower then he would chamois it down as soon as he returned home – day or night. He was also very emotional about scratches. Once, on a camping holiday in Cornwall when the bus had to stay in the car park, he sat up every night on guard duty. Imagine his despair when on the last night of the holiday it received a slight scratch on the driver door. One can only guess at the conversation in the family home the day when son Allan reversed it into a motorbike and put a tiny dent into the engine lid.

In 1975, when the eldest daughter went to college in Durham, Ray decided the camper was no longer big enough for them all to sleep in when picking her up at vacation time. He therefore took the bus back to Devon HQ in Sidmouth and had an elevating roof with hammock bunks fitted at a cost of £195. But the bunks were only ever used once or twice.

Sadly, in 1985 Ray suffered a stroke and the camper went into storage in his garage. In 2004 his wife, Brenda, died and, just eighteen days later, Ray joined her. And so 'the Volkswagen' passed to the safekeeping of their son Allan, something that had been decided long before. Allan initially had some problems moving the camper, which had been standing for nearly twenty years – the brakes had seized and the engine would not turn over. However, the brakes were freed by simply rocking the vehicle back and forth, some oil was dripped into the piston chambers and the engine was hand-cranked round by turning the pulley. A new battery was fitted, the key turned and bingo – the engine fired up first time on twenty-year-old petrol. Now that's a VW for you!

Because Ray had cared for his camper so lovingly, everything is still as it was: apart from slightly faded paint in a few areas, it's as if it had just rolled out of the VW showroom. The interior is pristine and even includes the original matching plastic washing bowl in the sink, the original melamine crockery set, the stainless steel cutlery set in its original plastic storage case and the awning in its original box. The elevating roof mechanism is as good as the day it was fitted and there is not a blemish or scratch to be found on the cabinetwork and upholstery. One feature not found on most campers of the time was a demountable oven – something even Volkswagen's brand-new T5 camper does not have.

With just 42,073 miles from new, it would be hard to find such a perfect example in terms of both body condition and original features and fittings. Allan now takes 'the Volkswagen' to the shows, where it has rightly won many awards for its immaculate, original condition. People are fascinated by the period features and layout, and Allan enjoys talking about and sharing the camper with others. While he has no plans to use it as a camper any more, he is determined to keep it in this condition as a tribute to his father. Despite receiving some lucrative offers to sell the camper, he intends to continue enjoying driving it and savouring the appreciation of others.

IT'S IN THE BLOOD

Ray, Brenda and their daughter Kathleen with the camper on its very first outing, in Sunderland in 1969.

The only time the awning was ever set up! Brenda, Kathleen and Allan, Sunderland, 1969.

Since coming out of retirement, the camper has won awards at every show it has attended.

THREE GENERATIONS

In 1958 Roy Caygill set up Eclipse Conversions, kitting out VW panel vans as campers. Having previously been a cabinetmaker and coach finisher for the British Rail Carriage and Wagon Works in Derby, as well as having a passion for engines and mechanicals, Roy was ideally suited to provide people with affordable, well-equipped campers. As he used panel vans as the base, he had to fit windows himself, using his own handmade fibreglass frames. However, this did provide a blank canvas inside, from which to design and build his own camping interiors. As time went on, he converted more and more vans to individual orders – and he even made his own fibreglass elevating roofs. By the late 1960s he had moved on to converting Commers and Transits, before losing his premises in the 70s and winding up the business.

Roy bought his first van in 1959 and converted it himself. He used this as a family camper for four years, and even drove it to Wolfsburg (the birthplace of the VW bus). Roy was quite a character. As well as racing motorcycles in the 1950s, he also had a passion for flying, and after reading an article about a gyrocopter in an American magazine, he set about building his own. He built this amazing machine from scratch in his garage and taught himself to fly it by reading a book. (A similar machine was used by James Bond, many years later, in the film *You Only Live Twice*.) He used to ferry the machine around by strapping it to the roof of his camper – which must have caused some confusion to other motorists.

Roy's children, Gail and Gary, had many happy family holidays in the camper, often joined by other family members. One of Gail's clearest memories is when, as a young girl, she became confused when her newlywed elder sister and new husband, who were travelling in convoy, inexplicably 'disappeared' for several hours en route to the campsite – it was several years before she realised that campers had other uses than just a family holiday!

Years spent growing up around a workshop outfitting VW campers, plus all those formative family holidays, meant it was inevitable that Gary would be into VWs. He saved hard to buy his first camper, finally managing it in 1994, when he bought a bus in need of 'serious restoration'. Gary was in no hurry, however, and spent five years working on his project bus, determined to make it into a show winner. This meant hours trawling the shows collecting all the parts he needed. He carried out all the work himself, basically rebuilding the whole bottom twelve inches all round. He also sprayed the camper in its original colours of turquoise and white. Sadly, Roy died from a form of asbestosis in 1996, aged just sixty-four, before he could see all the work Gary was doing to carry on the family tradition. Even more tragic is that he had contracted the disease after exposure to asbestos dust while working as a coach finisher, in the days before the world had woken up to the dangers of asbestos. Though it affected the family badly, Gary was determined to press on and finish the bus as a tribute to his dad, who had encouraged him throughout.

One tragedy is bad enough, but the Caygill family then received a double whammy. Totally out of the blue, Gary suffered a sudden, fatal heart attack just before Easter 1999, aged just thirty-four. The family were devastated but were equally determined that Gary's work should not be in vain. Gail was by then married to John Gerrard and had a son, Sam, aged five. The family all agreed that the camper should go to Sam, the next male in the Caygill line. John himself took on the daunting project of finishing the restoration and ensuring the work was of the high standard that Gary would have wanted.

For the next eight months John spent every evening and weekend working on the camper. John's knowledge of VWs was limited to having once helped change a Beetle engine, and it was quite a jigsaw trying to work out what all the pieces were that Gary had collected, and where to fit some of them. Putting the interior back together was a particular nightmare. John had to rebuild the engine Gary had acquired, refit the whole interior, source missing parts, and even French polish all the woodwork himself. As the camper neared completion, Gail made up a set of cushion and seat covers and curtains to match the exterior colours, and the camper finally hit the streets in July 2000.

In August that year the camper won both 'Restoration of the Year' (judged by a panel) and 'Van of the Year' (voted for by club members) at the Splitscreen Van Club's annual rally. Gail and John could hardly believe it, but were honoured to have fulfilled Gary's dream. Over the next few years the bus won awards at every show where it was displayed, and Gail, John and Sam enjoyed holidays and weekends in it. John and Gail are now very active committee members of the Splitscreen Van Club. Although they have progressed to a motorhome for their family holidays, the Split camper is still their pride and joy. As for Sam, he is now twelve and looking forward to the day when he will be able to drive the camper and discover its versatility and 'pulling power' for himself.

Opposite above: Roy and his hand-built gyrocopter.
Opposite left: The Caygill clan used always to camp together in the 1960s.
Opposite right: Roy outside the Eclipse workshop in the early 60s.

HAPPY FAMILIES

There's an old saying that 'the family that plays together stays together' and the Emmett family are a case in point. The only splits in this family are the Splits they drive. Father Brian, son Paul, and son-in-law Mark each own a Split camper that they are passionate about, but the buses are as individual as their owners. Ranging from totally stock to radical custom, the campers reflect their owners' differing needs, personalities and tastes. With wives and children, this extended family travels to shows together, goes on holiday together and can't begin to imagine living without their buses.

Paul Emmett is the one responsible for the family's VW bus obsession. He bought a 1972 Beetle when he was just fifteen, and spent two years restoring it before progressing to buses. He then restored, repainted and refurbished a 1963 Split camper, which he was very happy with – until he saw a 1959 23-window Samba Deluxe for sale at the Stanford Hall show in Leicestershire in spring 2004. This was a major turning point for the whole family. In order to buy it, he sold his orange and black Split to his brother-in-law Mark and then helped his parents track down and buy a fully original, completely restored Devon camper. Brian and his wife, Sue, having seen the pleasure and fun their grown-up children and their grandchildren were having with their campers, had decided they just had to be part of it, too. Brian has always had an interest in classic cars, and so when Paul told him of a mint, original-condition Devon camper for sale, the die was cast.

'Sally', as the bus is called, had been converted by Devon in 1963 and, after four owners, she was finally, in 1994, parked in a garden where she was used as a 'summerhouse'. By the time enthusiast Phil Thomas heard of her, she was in quite poor condition and moss had gathered on every flat surface, which had lifted the paint, causing

oxidisation to set in. Surprisingly, however, the interior remained complete and in excellent condition throughout. Even the original crockery and cutlery set was still intact. After a full restoration, which took three years, Phil reluctantly had to part with the camper. Enter Brian.

What is so special about this camper is that everything is just about as it was when it left the

Devon factory in 1963: curtains, upholstery, crockery, furniture, Dudley cooker – the works. Stock, original campers are a constant source of delight for bus owners, and this example is one of the best there is, having already won many awards. For Brian and Sue, their Devon gives them the chance 'to enjoy weekends out with the family and also parking up at shows where we can talk to people and enjoy their reactions to the originality of the bus'.

Opposite: Sealing Wax Red and Beige Grey is a classic VW colour scheme.
Top left: Crockery and cooker cabinets are mounted on the load doors.
Below left: This was the only Devon Caravette model to feature a sink and pump tap.
Right: The interior is in original condition, including upholstery and curtains.

When Paul saw the 1959 Samba Deluxe for sale at Stanford Hall, he realised its potential and just knew he had to have it. Having restored and customised a camper already, he had plenty of ideas about what he wanted to do with his new project. All the metalwork had already been done, including a complete rebuild of the bottom six inches, and £9,000 had been spent on the bodywork alone. 'It just needed an interior and paint,' says Paul.

Paul wanted to create something that looked close to original but with a modern twist. This decided the colour scheme – the original classic Sealing Wax Red and Beige Grey colours were given a contemporary look by using modern metallic and pearlescent paints. For the interior he built a bulkhead cabinet in maple veneered MDF to house the cooker, heater, gas bottle and storage. He then got Bernard Newbury, whose innovative and excellent car interiors have won many prizes at shows, to design and trim the interior to complement the look. This included new headliner, door cards, cushions, sunroof, cab carpet and cab seats and matching buttoned upholstery for the new rock-and-roll bed. The colours complement the exterior paint perfectly, creating a light, harmonised modern look while still retaining a period feel.

He didn't stop there, however. Owners love accessories for their campers, and Paul's camper boasts Porsche Fuchs wheels, a Westfalia roof rack, a Mota-Lite steering wheel, front safari windows, drop-down roof-mounted ten-inch DVD screen (great for the kids on long journeys), leisure battery/split charger, speakers, interior lights, cigarette lighter, LED indicators built into the rear lights, US-spec headlights and extra gauges fitted into the fresh air intake box. The end result is stunning, and Paul has certainly achieved his aim of a modern interpretation of a classic look. He says it is a fantastic vehicle to drive and he loves the attention and interest such an individual and quirky look creates. As well as taking the family out nearly every weekend, the bus also makes for the perfect family holiday.

Opposite above: Original VW colours have been given a modern twist.

Opposite left: Maple cabinets house the cooker and provide kitchen storage.

Opposite right: A drop down DVD player is the perfect solution to the 'Are we there yet?' syndrome.

Right: The Deluxe Microbus, commonly known as the Samba, has roof lights and a sliding roof. Opening safari windscreens are the ultimate cool accessory.

When Mark Forton married into the Emmett family, VW buses were already in his blood. He has long been a VW bus lover and he even works for VW Commercial as a national rental manager, so he gets to drive and talk buses at work as well as play. When Paul put his 1963 orange and black Split camper up for sale to finance the 1959 Samba Deluxe project, Mark immediately took it on, as it was in much better shape than his '67 Devon, and much more practical for the family. Plus there was the bonus of knowing what his brother-in-law had done to the camper already.

Paul had spent a lot of time and effort in getting the bus right. As well as the distinctive custom black under orange paintwork, the bus came with a fitted DIY interior that sleeps four (complete with drop-down screen DVD player), gas heating, Empi five-spoke wheels, side step, US-style indicators in the headlights, red rear lenses and a Scat shifter gearstick. The bus also features opening windows all round – front safaris, six opening side pop-outs and an opening rear window: the ultimate in cool.

Since acquiring the bus, Mark has fitted a fully detailed and chromed 1641cc engine. Like the others, Mark drives around with a permanent smile on his face, and the distinctive paint scheme means the bus always gets noticed.

Despite their love of classic Splitscreen Campers, Paul and Mark now own T25 Campers as they find them more practical, comfortable and family friendly. But the Emmett family will always be a VW Camper family!

Right: The DIY interior follows traditional designs.
Opposite top: Six opening side windows, a safari opening rear window and a side step are all period accessories.
Opposite bottom left: The orange and black paint scheme is very distinctive.
Opposite bottom right: A cooker/grill has been sited at the side of the rear seat.

As well as travelling together to shows, where they love talking about their buses and looking at other people's buses, the Emmett family use their campers for exactly what they were designed to do – and most weekends they will be out somewhere for a picnic or drive, turning heads in the process. To protect the fronts from the dreaded stone chips, Sue even made each bus a personalised bus bib, matching the colours of the bus and adding the bus's name.

3 OVERLAND WITH THE OBERLANDERS

By the early 1960s the VW campervan had already established its credentials for overland adventures; as mentioned in the Introduction, the very first Westfalia VW camper had travelled round South Africa in 1953. Even so, travelling in South America was like exploring one of the last wild places – terrible roads (which more often than not were just tracks), political instability, civil war, deep-seated corruption and nightmare bureaucracy being just some of things that have not changed. Embarking on a road trip there today is scary enough, but this family's story takes place in 1965, when aptly named Helmut and Nelly Oberlander took their three young children on an epic trip clocking up 25,000 miles in just seven months. Cris Torlasco, founder of Wet Westies, was so inspired by the story of their exploits that he undertook a similar trip in 2003. He spent a lot of time with the Oberlanders, and, thanks to him, their story can at last be shared.

Helmut and Nelly Oberlander were happy to share photos, stories, and even 16mm film about their epic trip. 'We thought it was a good idea to do this before getting old', said Nelly. Their German accent is still heavy, even after forty-eight years in the United States. They can't help showing a bit of nostalgia as the old Leitz projects their wonderful slides. In the meantime, Helmut mentions his lifetime involvement with VWs, starting in 1945 as an apprentice mechanic in Germany (before VW buses were around), training at the VW Wolfsburg factory in 1957 and eventually moving to the United States, where he worked for the

VW dealerships Riviera Motors and Gateway Volkswagen in Portland, Oregon. After many years with VW, he opened his own shop in Eugene, Oregon. Now in his seventies, Helmut still repairs and rebuilds VW air-cooled engines in the same building.

The Oberlanders started dreaming of a trip through the Americas in December 1964. The family owned a 1959 dove blue panel bus that they had bought secondhand in 1961. They prepared for the adventure conscientiously, writing to every consulate, finding a ship that would take their bus from Panama to Colombia (there being no road for part of the way between Central and South America) and gathering as much information as possible. This was a hard task. Helmut recalls calling the American Automobile Association to get general information and acquire the Carnet de Passage, a bond document required by several Latin American countries. The AAA clerk responded with a categorical 'Don't do it', adding in an alarming voice, 'too dangerous' and 'almost impossible'. Coming from someone in the travel industry, it was definitely not encouraging.

Finally, on 23rd March 1965, Helmut, Nelly and their daughters Ingrid, Christine and Doris, aged ten, five and three, set off, with the milometer reading 53,073 miles. They headed south, a course they wouldn't abandon for the next four months. In four days they were entering Mexico through Nogales, and six days later they were in Mexico City. 'We were independent, and our camper was our home,' says Helmut.

Previous pages, from left to right:
A map drawn on the camper recorded their route.
At 10,000 feet the air is bright, but very cold.
At every township locals thronged around to smile and stare.

Sand blowing across the road made driving difficult in Chile.
A typical roadside scene.
Opposite: Outside Nelly's parents' house in southern Brazil.

Unloading in Columbia.

Flooded roads on the Ecuador / Peru border.

The only way the camper negotiated mud-choked roads in Argentina was with snow chains.

Ready to be freighted by rail over the Andes to Argentina.

Typical Andean scenes.

The Inca ruins of Machu Picchu.

Cris and his family, with Helmut and Nelly, pictured outside Helmut's workshop in 2005.

By 7th April they were in Guatemala. The temperature inside the bus registered 110°F. On the 10th of that month they crossed the border with El Salvador. Then came Honduras, where they had the first flat tyre of many to come. Later that month they drove through Nicaragua, Costa Rica and Panama, where they got stopped by the police – for driving without a shirt. In Panama City, they had to endure bureaucratic delays related to shipping the bus to Colombia, so they took advantage of the two-week wait by getting to know Panama. Finally, on 30th April 1965, they boarded the ship that would take them and their bus to Buenaventura, Colombia.

From Colombia they drove through Ecuador, where crossing the equator was, of course, a milestone in their trip. At the border between Ecuador and Peru they bumped into a river crossing that had lost its bridge to the floods, but the locals put them and their bus on a banana raft and they made it into Peru. They crossed northern Chile (one of the driest places on the planet) successfully. 'At one point, we drove 220 miles through desert land with nothing in between,' remembers Helmut. 'No humans, no vegetation, no animals, nothing.'

Then came the scariest moment in the whole trip. Since they had to wait almost a day for the train that would take them across the Andes to Argentina, Helmut and Nelly went to get some supplies in Santiago de Chile. The bus was already loaded on the flatbed train car, and the three children stayed inside, with instructions not to leave the vehicle at any time. Several hours later, both parents came back, and to their shock the train was gone. In desperation, they started asking around, and the first response was that the train had already left for Argentina. After further frantic enquiries, however, they were told that the train had only been moved to another location within the yard, and they were reunited with their children and the bus. After that, they boarded the train and crossed the Andes mountain range into Argentina, with temperatures below freezing and deep snow.

On 3rd June the family reached Buenos Aires, the southernmost point in their journey, with the milometer showing 64,336 miles. They then headed to the Iguazu Falls in north-east Argentina, which they describe as 'the mightiest waterfall in the world'. The road became extremely muddy for two whole days before they got to the falls. At one point, the bus lost one of the snow chains that were used for traction in the mud. Noticing this, Helmut retraced the bus's tracks, walking through the deep mud, till he found the missing chain about a mile back. Once in Iguazu, the family stayed at the only campsite they found in all of Central and South America.

After visiting the falls, the Oberlanders headed to neighbouring Brazil, where Nelly had relatives. Bureaucratic issues forced them to smuggle the bus into the country, pretending it was an Argentinian vehicle that came from the town of Oregon, in Argentina. They visited the then new modernist city of Brasilia, deep in the jungle. Their slides show dozens of Split Window buses and Bugs driving the Brazilian streets. Helmut notes that these were Brazilian-made. Parts for their bus were, not surprisingly, abundant.

The bus then took them back to Argentina, and later Bolivia as they headed back north. In Bolivia they reached the highest altitude of the trip: 16,800 feet above sea level at the Chacaltaya astronomical observatory. The bus lost all power due to the altitude, stalling at the observatory's entrance. The whole family spent the night there, in extremely low temperatures. Helmut remembers waking up the next morning and finding their bottled water, which had been inside the bus at all times, completely frozen. When they tried to light their cooking stove, the matches were not working. Helmut realised it was because of the lack of oxygen owing to the high altitude and their own consumption during the night. As soon as he opened some windows, the matches worked. From then on, they slept with one window open, no matter what the temperature.

The Oberlanders visited La Paz (at about 12,000 feet above sea level it is the highest capital city in the world) and then crossed the famous Lake Titicaca into Peru. Here, because of the high altitude, the three girls and Nelly had to push the powerless bus uphill. After visiting Cuzco and the nearby Inca city of Machu Picchu, they headed north, retracing their previous route.

Throughout the trip, the Oberlanders visited museums and archaeological sites. They slept at ranches, farms, churches and local people's houses. Beaches, car parks, customs buildings, petrol stations and even a Mennonite seminary served as occasional shelters. But the safest place, they add, was always the local cemetery, 'since locals do not like to be that close to the dead'. Asked about mechanical problems experienced with the bus along the trip, Helmut casually replies, 'None whatsoever, not even minor ones. We did get about ten flat tyres.' He also mentions taking a spare carburettor set up for driving at high altitudes, and performing several tune-ups along the way.

On 1st November 1965, the Oberlanders parked the bus, which was filled to the roof with souvenirs, in their driveway in Oregon. They had successfully completed the loop: 25,517 miles in seven months and eight days, averaging twenty miles per US gallon. These days, Helmut and Nelly stay busy boating, dancing the polka, attending beer festivals, travelling to Germany – and keeping old VWs alive. Good thing they are doing all of that now, 'before they get old'!

Story courtesy Cris Torlasco

The Volkswagen Camper

**OLDSWORTHS have
e reputation**

Our home on the range

For the past fifty years, the ability to go where you please and when you please has been an enduring theme in VW camper advertising – even the new VW T5 camper brochure uses a shot of the van against a backdrop of wilderness and mountains as its main image to capture the essence of life with a campervan. Brochure shots have always emphasised the outdoor life, showing families or couples relaxing and enjoying themselves in scenic locations. What is especially interesting is the way the brochure pictures over time have become period social documents that capture the changing aspirations, fashions and lifestyles of five decades. Yet they have one common element: people getting together to have fun away from the stress of daily life. The clothes, hairstyles and interior fabrics and colours may change, but living with a VW camper is always about fun, freedom and individuality. The appeal of the VW camper has always been the ability to realise the dream of getting away from it all and being yourself.

In 1955 Westfalia introduced the first fully fitted-out campers and captured the essence of what life with a VW camper was all about:

Volkswagen Kombi with Westfalia de Luxe Camping Equipment

Presented by:

Make more of your leisure and your holidays –
the VW Kombi with Westfalia de Luxe Camping Equipment
opens a whole new field of intriguing possibilities!
We should be glad to send you full particulars.
Just drop us a line.

Westfalia Werke KG · Wiedenbrück/Westf. [Germany] · Tel. 240

The manufacturer reserves the right to change illustrations and specifications. Printed in Germany.

'Don't you sometimes long to leave life's hurly-burly behind you and go out into the wide world and pause in woods and meadows, by inviting lakes and hills, to camp where the restraining arm of civilisation cannot reach you? With the Westfalia Deluxe Camping Equipment you can transform your dreams into wonderful reality, giving you the chance of exploring nature's nooks and crannies, exchanging the bustle of the main road for the windings of a country lane... This holiday home on wheels will transform the world into an exciting picture book for you where every page is a new and satisfying experience.'

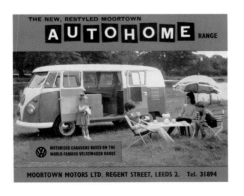

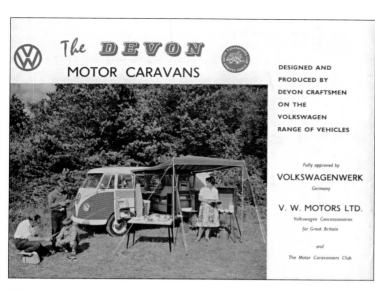

The DEVON
MOTOR CARAVANS

DESIGNED AND
PRODUCED BY
DEVON CRAFTSMEN
ON THE
VOLKSWAGEN
RANGE OF VEHICLES

Fully approved by

VOLKSWAGENWERK
Germany

V. W. MOTORS LTD.
Volkswagen Concessionaires
for Great Britain

and

The Motor Caravanners Club

Boudoir ♥

This is the master bedroom. Big double bed, six feet long (we can make it a foot more if you wish) and five inches of deep foam mattress.
There's a stereo system for mood music and a radio to keep you in touch with civilisation.
There are optional bunks in the elevating roof and cab and a super Isabella side tent which will sleep three adults – free standing of course.

Despite its image as a hippie vehicle, the VW camper was actually the province of the newly affluent middle class in society. In 1963 Dormobile captured the aspirations and lifestyle of middle England with this description of its vehicle's benefits:

'As well as being an ideal home on wheels, it is a mobile grandstand at races, sports meetings, gymkhanas and other outdoor displays of all kinds. If the weather is unkind, the huge roof windows give an excellent viewpoint, refreshments are laid on and the radio is an optional extra.'

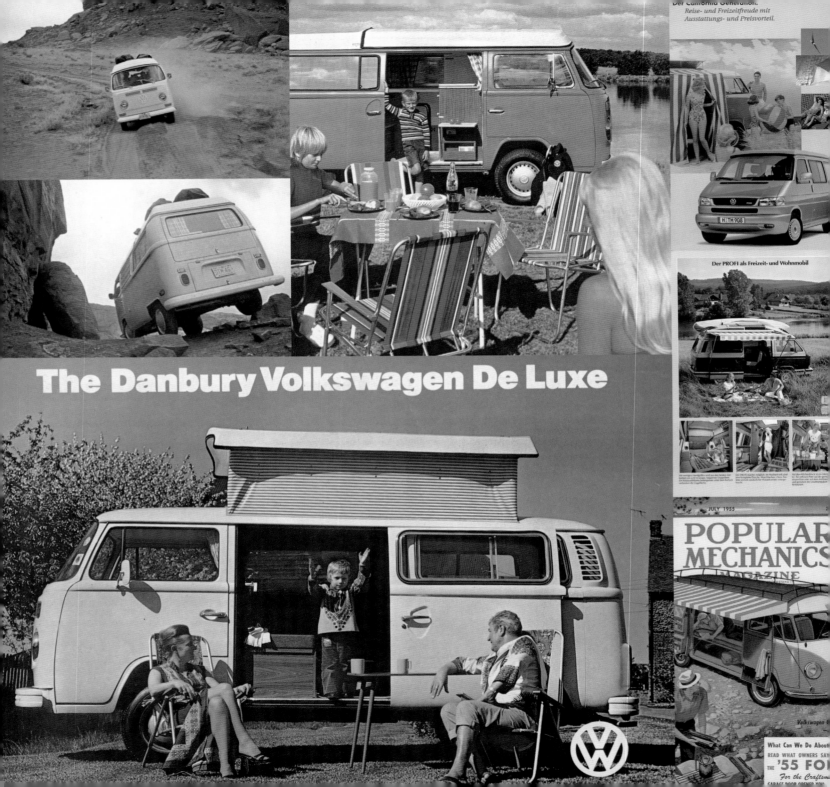

The Danbury Volkswagen De Luxe

The VW camper's other appeal lay in its versatility, so that it could be both a family vehicle and a camper. Danbury literature of 1969 emphasised these multi-purpose features:

'Danbury conversions offer you the best of both worlds. An economical vehicle for everyday use with built-in comfort and unequalled mobility… ideal for town or country. PLUS all the amenities of a luxury caravan. Now the Danbury offers 'Forward Facing Seats' – do away with that crick in the neck – here is the opportunity to go where and when you please in comfort.'

Other companies preferred to concentrate on space and luxury, as in this 1971 Viking advert:

Viking. So much more than a Volkswagen. Viking is an entirely new concept in motor caravan design and its versatile use of space, ingenious design and superb quality put it ahead of the field – in every field. There's room for everything in a Viking. Room for lounging and dining. Room for cooking and loving. And a separate room for the children.

By 1973 Volkswagen AG had granted exclusive conversion licences to Westfalia and Devon, and were warning buyers of the potential dangers of buying a non-VW-approved conversion. Viking fought back, using the freedom and individuality symbolised by a VW camper; the little person up against the corporate conglomerate:

The Viking invaders have arrived. The biggest battle in motor caravan history has begun. It will be hard. It will be long. And you are a witness. Viking Motorhomes on one side; Devon and Westfalia on the other. David and Goliath all over again. You were born to be free. You buy a motor caravan to stay free. Your freedom gives you the

right to choose. Before you buy, insist on seeing a Viking. We'll send a Viking to your door. If you're sure it's what you want we'll build one just for you. One more Viking on our side. One more blow for freedom.

Devon brochures of the mid 70s continued to emphasise the multipurpose uses of a VW bus, summing up the appeal of their latest Caravette model as follows:

Our camper is not just a camper. It's whatever you want it to be. A roomy estate car or a minibus, a runabout for picking up the kids or the shopping. You might think that is enough for any car, not so with this one. When other cars finish this VW begins. It can be your English country cottage or your villa in some sun-drenched foreign part. And unlike any cottage or villa you can pack up and go, anywhere you like, whenever you like. A VW Camper is built to work hard and play hard – taking the children to school or play, for going fishing or to the races, collecting gardening materials – in fact any of the 1001 uses that our estate car has been designed to do. And after your motor caravan has spent the day working hard, it too likes the special evening out. To the theatre, the ballet or the opera and perhaps, afterwards, an extra special candlelit dinner. Truly a car for all occasions.

No mention of surfers or the alternative culture here!

By the 1980s campervan buyers wanted that bit more comfort and a higher level of equipment as standard, though the spirit of adventure was still the key selling point. Westfalia recognised the changing times and desires:

Adventure with comfort? Yes, it's here at last and no longer just for armchair travellers… The VW

Camper has brought the comfortable, yet unconventional, holiday within your reach.

With a VW camper you can move away from the safe and known, and access a simpler world, a more exciting world where you have control over your destiny. Such dreams are an essential part of the human psyche, and advertisers know exactly which buttons to press.

5 WIDE-EYED WANDERERS

Previous pages, from left to right:
Amanda continued her yoga practice throughout the journey.
View of Tierra del Fuego.
Journey's end – the tip of South America.
A herd of llama blocks the road in the Andes of northern Peru.
Easter Island is part of Chile – a last-minute flight from Santiago allowed a brief visit to this eerie and remote spot.

In 2001 Amanda and Richard Ligato quit their American Dream lifestyle, which offered security, certainty, comfort… and boredom. Everything was just that bit too easy and safe; there was no risk in their lives. Much to the astonishment (and envy) of their friends and colleagues, they quit their jobs, gave up their nice house and gave away most of the material clutter that had once seemed important. They bought a 1978 Westfalia camper and spent the next three years travelling through Mexico, Central and South America and Africa. Amanda is Mexican, while Richard describes himself as a typical gringo, and as an interracial couple they had always sought to blend both cultures into their marriage. Hoping to learn more about themselves on their journey, they would find their patience tested to the limits in the months and years ahead.

The following extracts have been taken from *Wide-Eyed Wanderers, A Befuddling Journey from the Rat Race to the Roads of Latin America and Africa*, the book they wrote chronicling their exploits. It is available from Pop-Top Publishing at www.VWVagabonds.com. The Ligatos covered over 60,000 miles – probably an unofficial world record – exploring life on the road and, in the process, discovered first-hand how others find joy in life.

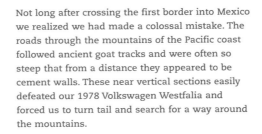

Amanda with a young boy at Lake Titicaca, Peru.

Not long after crossing the first border into Mexico we realized we had made a colossal mistake. The roads through the mountains of the Pacific coast followed ancient goat tracks and were often so steep that from a distance they appeared to be cement walls. These near vertical sections easily defeated our 1978 Volkswagen Westfalia and forced us to turn tail and search for a way around the mountains.

In frustration I would curse my stupidity. Before leaving home, Amanda and I knew we would encounter difficult roads. Problem was, we did not know a whole lot about the internal workings of the Volkswagen. In our ignorance we had a mechanic change the van's original high-powered motor with a lower power but less complicated Beetle motor. The Volkswagen Beetle has infested nearly every corner of the globe. It seemed a good idea to give up sheer power for versatility and everyone said the Beetle motor was simple enough to repair, even for an idiot like me.

We had bought the van from a burned out ex-hippie in the southern Californian town of Ocean Beach. Despite being 'altitude challenged' the van putted around Mexico for nearly six months, taking us to the Day of the Dead celebrations in Pátzcuaro, the spectacular monarch butterfly migration in the mountains of Morelia, the European migration to the nude beaches of Zipolite, and the remote indigenous villages of Chiapas. Sputtering headlong into the sediment bowl capital Mexico City, where the thick smog makes Los Angeles seem pollution free, we fought with buses, taxis and maniacal drivers to find the basilica of the Virgin of Guadalupe, the patron saint of Mexico, for her celebration day along with eight million pilgrims.

Through Central America the heat was oppressive, and we had just a small 12-volt fan to blow the clammy air around in circles as we slept in the pop-top roof. At night during the tropical rain we were forced to zip closed the opening on the rooftop tent to keep out the pounding drops. It began to feel as if we were living within a soggy plastic bag. A few days of this and the inside of the pop-top sprouted a gray fuzzy mold. Like a clean freak Michelangelo, Amanda would lie on her back with rubber gloves, bleach, and a sponge, scouring the inside of the roof raw. We hung our wet laundry inside the van but it absolutely refused to dry. The only way we could free ourselves from the constant humidity was to remain in motion. When driving, a current of air streamed in through the jalousie windows, catching everything in a whirlwind, fluttering the moist clothing and swirling gusts into the damp corners.

While searching for a place to stay in the jungles of Costa Rica we found a grassy lawn that an enterprising local had turned into a makeshift campsite on the slopes of a dormant volcano. Reaching high into the atmosphere, the volcano created a strange funnel effect, driving clouds with precipitation directly over us. The rain fell hard and the massive drops pelted the roof of the van with a deafening drumming. As I climbed up to bed after a tiring day of driving I noticed water seeping through the canvas siding of the van's tent roof. Amanda quickly grabbed a rag and wiped the droplets from the inside. As she dabbed at the material a violent wind struck the van and the canvas let out a loud, zipping 'snap', splitting into a two-foot-long tear. We both stared at the opening in disbelief as the rain poured in on our bed.

Heading south on the Pan American Highway through Guatemala, Honduras, Nicaragua, Costa Rica and Panama we were using a horrible map we had picked up for free from the Auto Club. The scale was so small that one inch equaled a whopping 145 miles of land. Any useful features like mile markers, intersecting roads, small towns, rivers, lakes, mountains, bridges, anything that could help pinpoint our position, was not indicated.

Every so often I glanced over at Amanda, the navigator, and became irritated as I discovered our only map, unreliable as it was, taped to her window as a sunshade, or spread out on her lap as a food tray. She would fold it into a fancy fan to get relief from the sweltering heat or roll it into a baton and use it as a fly swatter. It never failed to amaze me how it could morph into some absurd gadget rendering it temporarily off-limits at the precise moment I needed directions. To bring her back to reality I would ask through gritted teeth, 'Uh, how many more kilometers, do you think?' She would shrug, tap the bobbing compass on the dashboard and answer unconcernedly, 'We're going south.'

As we continued on the journey and got farther away from our uptight world, I learned to concentrate less on how we got to where we were, or the route we would take to leave. I began to enjoy the world, not in the way a map shows, but quite the opposite, by experiencing one place at a time. Rather than looking to what was next, or to what had been, I began to enjoy a place and time Amanda knew well, living in the now.

A roadside waterfall in Costa Rica.

Worried chickens look on while Richard prepares a meal.

A village in northern Mexico ready for Independence Day celebrations.

Hand-cranked car ferry in Belize.

Then we reached the end of the road. In southern Panama there is one small stretch where the road is nonexistent. The break is at the remote strip of jungle where Central and South America are linked, a place called the Darién Gap. It seems absurd that nearly 18,000 miles of road and two geographically connected continents are kept apart by a tiny, almost insignificant morsel. The impenetrable fifty-four-mile gap lies between the towns of Yaviza, Palo de Las Letras in Panama and Mutatá in Colombia.

To escape the persistent mosquitoes, the awning was draped with material used for making wedding veils.

With no road to go on, the undeterred pair decided to ship their vehicle to South America. Getting their vehicle onto a ship was easy, but getting it back proved much more difficult, and only bribes secured its release. Once the van was secured, they continued their interrupted drive:

On the Central Route, surrounded by banana plantations and palm trees, we stopped by the side of the road near Santo Domingo de Los Colorados at the foothills of the Andes to make adjustments to the van. I had a basic understanding of the workings of the Volkswagen motor. I knew that the gas exploded inside somewhere and that the explosions were converted into motion. On the practical side of things, I could change the spark plugs and the oil, and follow the tedious directions to adjust the valves, because everyone said, 'You gotta adjust the valves.' I had no idea why the valves needed adjustment, no clue how they got out of adjustment, in fact I did not know what the valves did, but I routinely lay down under the rear end of the van every 1,500 miles and adjusted them with a greasy discomfort.

Our library in the van included the book *How to Keep Your Volkswagen Alive, a Manual of Step–by-Step Procedures by the Complete Idiot*, written in the sixties and seventies by a hippie couple who understood the value of learning from experience. 'The Idiot's Guide', as we affectionately called it, starts from scratch, assuming that the reader knows absolutely nothing. Front is front. The left of the car is the driver's side and the engine is in the rear. Slowly, methodically, Amanda read the procedure from the book as I worked. We made some minor adjustments that somehow, mysteriously, gave the van more power as we headed up into the thinner air.

And then came the police of Peru. Shortly after crossing the border we began a song and dance routine that we repeated fourteen times in the first week alone. A Peruvian police officer would be leaning against his shiny new Toyota Land Cruiser, concealing his face behind aviator sunglasses. He would lazily stroll to the center of the two-lane highway and signal us to move off to the side of the road. The conversations would always begin cordially, 'Buenas tardes'. Then the officer would create some absurd infraction. 'Señor, you were driving at 110 kilometers per hour. The speed limit here is 50.' Politely I would deny it. 'No Oficial, no es posible. The van can only go as fast as 80. It has never gone up to 110.' Amanda would smile and say, 'Oh no. We respect your laws. We would never disobey them.'

One officer said, 'You obviously do not respect our laws because your license plate is in the wrong place.' Another demanded, 'You were going over the white line.' A third averted his eyes and alleged, 'You did not use your turn signal.' We hadn't turned for a hundred miles. With each accusation the officers became just a bit ruder and more abrasive, and we in turn became more polite and friendly. Amanda would use flattery and say, 'It's always a pleasure meeting the honest police officers of Peru.' They would grumble and we would smile. After a while they would conclude that we were not as fearful as they had hoped and would deduce that we would probably not be making a contribution to their lunch fund.

The encounters had me so rattled that I searched for a very American solution to the problem. I paged through a local phonebook and jotted down the phone number of the Peruvian Transit Police in Lima. I wrote it on a sticky-note with the words 'Police Corruption Unit' written across the top in

Spanish and stuck it to the back of my driver's license. We continued to be pulled over. By the time we reached Nazca in southern Peru we had lost count at fifty. I still got the same jolt each time it happened, but we became quite skilled at repeating the script. In the end my confidence grew and I felt satisfaction in knowing that we had never resorted to giving a bribe to the police.

When summer arrived we turned south to Argentina and Route 40 through Patagonia. Over time, the dirt and gravel roads formed corrugations on the surface, like waves that grew into ruts just a few inches apart. These rutted sections were tortuous. They ate away our tires, burned up our shock absorbers, jangled every nut, bolt, electrical connection, fuel line, and fastener, causing the van's most unexpected parts to wobble loose. It vibrated every fiber of our being, exhausting my arms and hands from gripping the steering wheel, rattling our teeth and numbing our butts. The dust was unbelievable, penetrating keyholes, cabinets, bedding, clothing, food, ears, and nose. At the end of one of these sections we looked like two doughnuts coated with powdered sugar. Each day after driving I would spend an hour checking the connections, tightening bolts and replugging wires, while Amanda pulled everything out of the inside of the van, and swept, dusted, and shook the dirt off. One afternoon I found a loose shock-absorber. Another day the muffler hung on by a thread. Had a part fallen off, broken, or failed in the middle of nowhere, with no traffic and little hope of getting to a town, it would not have been good.

When driving slowly on these corrugated roads we dipped into each of the ruts, then rolled over the high point, down again then up again, certainly easier on the car, but a thousand miles at ten miles an hour was out of the question. At mid-speed the wheels would dip to the low point in the ripple, then bang over the high point, killing the shocks and tires in the process. The only reasonable option was to drive like a madman. At high speed, over forty-five miles an hour, the tires jumped from the top of one mound to the next, skimming over the low points, minimizing the vibration at the expense of control. It felt like driving a boat. I would set a course in a particular direction and unseen factors would conspire against the steering. Suddenly the van would drift to the left or the right, ignoring my frantic wheel turning to the contrary. We drove down the center of the road to allow a margin of error. Every so often a car came in the other direction and we would slow down, moving as far to the right as possible to avoid being hit by flying rocks. The truck drivers didn't care, and operated at full speed, throwing rocks that pinged and dented the van and glanced off the windshield.

Just south of Ushuaia, a dirt road continues through Tierra del Fuego National Park and marks the end of road at the Beagle Channel. We drove the last few kilometers down this dusty track to the sign that read in Spanish, 'Here is the end of route number 3, Alaska 17,518 km.'

Standing in front of the sign waiting for Amanda to prop the camera on a log and set the automatic timer, I thought back to how I imagined this moment would be. Setting out on our journey, we wanted to learn the simple things for ourselves. We wanted to experience how people in other parts of the world live. We wondered if we could pick and choose some of their best characteristics and meld them into our lives.

Reaching the end of the road, we remained mystified by the dense complexity of what makes a life fulfilling. With each new lesson learned we succeeded in revealing how little we really knew. We could not completely grasp what it was in the lives of these Latinos that brought them joy and happiness, but we realized that prosperity seemed irrelevant.

Hugging Amanda close, smiling toward the camera with a goofy grin, I wondered how it was that we found happiness in the most unlikely place, living in the close quarters of a Volkswagen campervan for nearly a year and a half. But before going back home we needed a clearer understanding of the route we had taken to get there. Only then could we plot a course to the future. We had to go where it all began. We had to go to Africa...

Crossing the Peruvian desert.

The van often broke down and they learned how to repair it through trial and error. Here, Rich is struggling over a tune-up in Argentina.

After a further twelve months' travelling in and around Africa in their VW camper, Richard and Amanda finally arrived back in San Diego, having clocked up a staggering 59,405 miles. Life would never be the same again. As they drove once more on familiar roads, Richard summed up his thoughts:

We knew that no matter how much we wanted them to be, the mysterious elements that make us happy were not hidden in the dull everyday routines we created. That Christmas morning feeling, of being alive, vibrant, pulsating, came the moment we put ourselves beyond what was comfortable, what was familiar, what was known. In pressing on the accelerator to speed up and change lanes, I listened to the contented, whistling purr of the camper's exhaust. I knew the sound so well, like the beat of my own heart, and I could hear in it the faint difference between simply living and being alive.

Beach camping in Belize.

6 HIPPIE BUSES, HAPPY DAYS AND HOPE

The 1960s were a time of social upheaval and change. Students took over campuses, the streets of Paris saw workers and students marching arm in arm, anti-Vietnam War protesters placed flowers in the gun barrels of the onlooking National Guard, Pink Floyd played for free in Hyde Park, the Pink Fairies toured the streets playing from the back of a lorry... and those of us who were there really did believe we could change the world. They say if you can remember the '60s you weren't part of it, but that could not be more wrong.

Woodstock summed up the mood and feeling of a generation who could dream that the bombers riding shotgun in the skies could turn to butterflies, and that a world of peace and harmony was still possible. A press photographer at Woodstock snapped a shot of a couple listening to the music on the roof of their brightly painted VW camper, which was subsequently reproduced in many papers and magazines (and even figured on the Woodstock Album inner sleeve). For many, this shot summed up the atmosphere and spirit of the event, and the VW camper had its image changed for ever, as a new generation, who naïvely shouted about dying before they got old, claimed it as their own.

Alice's Restaurant was one of those seminal movies, like Easy Rider, that captured the changing lifestyle and mood of many young people in the late 60s. It loosely chronicled the story of a young Arlo Guthrie and his friends, and their encounters with authority, from draft dodging to hostile reactions to their appearance. Based on true events (there really was an old church that Alice planned to turn into a restaurant), it was also a gentle, bittersweet look at a time of growing awareness, protest and youth culture, including drugs. (While scenes of smoking dope were often comic, there was actually a powerful anti-hard-drugs subtext, as one of the characters dies from heroin use.) Central to the film was a sub-plot revolving round Arlo, a VW bus, dumped garbage and his subsequent arrest and trial for garbage dumping. Although movies like Woodstock had shown images of VW campers clogged in traffic, it was Alice's Restaurant that introduced many young people to the possibilities opened up by owning a

bus. This was no flower-power hippie bus, however – it was an immaculate red and white Deluxe Microbus (commonly known as a Samba), complete with sliding sunroof (perfect for throwing out garbage!). But its central role in a movie about young people and their dreams, fears and aspirations influenced a generation.

A second-hand VW bus was an ideal mode of transport for them, as it was practical, versatile, cheap to buy, easy to maintain and excellent for travelling with a group of friends. Old campers and buses could easily be picked up for just a couple of hundred pounds (or dollars) – who cared about shiny paint or powerful engines? For surfers it was the ideal vehicle to carry boards and sleep on the beach in; for music fans it was perfect to camp out in at a rock festival; for those wanting to travel overland it had already proved itself capable of coping with rough terrain and roads. A new generation now claimed the VW bus as their symbol of freedom, and its quaint, old-fashioned look just added to the appeal. The old 'holiday cottage on wheels' image was gradually eroded as more young people began to own and use the vehicle, even though the only ones they could afford were usually old, tatty and in need of TLC. No one would think of hand-painting a new camper, but a scruffy, cheap runabout presented the perfect blank canvas to express yourself on. And so the brightly coloured 'hippie bus' became synonymous with fun-loving, freewheeling good times.

The majority of these buses were not owned by true hippies, however – the new owners were the post-

Woodstock generation, chasing a fading dream. Of the many VW buses travelling the so called 'hippie trail' to India up to the late 1970s, very few were driven by hippies, unless the term means anyone wanting to opt out of the rat race, even temporarily. Despite this, over the years the image of the VW camper as a hippie bus has been cemented in the mind of the public. Countless movies, sitcoms and adverts have drawn on, and perpetuated, this romanticised, stereotypical view of the VW camper and its owners.

In the United States, however, the stereotype is more accurate, and it is here the true origins of the association between hippies and VW campers lie. The word hippie is commonly thought to have come from combining the words 'hip' and 'happy'; however, digging deeper, it is fascinating to discover that the Hopi indians had a prophecy, many hundreds of years old, that said a group of white-skinned people would bring back the ancient ways of peace and respect for Mother Earth. 'Hopi' means 'the peaceful people', so perhaps this is the true origin of the word.

Back in the early 1960s, Ken Kesey (author of One Flew Over the Cuckoo's Nest) and the Merry Pranksters had travelled around in brightly painted American schoolbuses with lurid and psychedelic artwork replacing the municipal yellow. It was the time of Timothy Leary, The Electric Kool-Aid Acid Test by Tom Wolfe and the motto 'Tune in, Turn on, Drop out', with LSD opening the doors of consciousness. The West Coast band the Grateful Dead spent time with Ken Kesey and the Pranksters and had a unique

Previous pages, from left to right:
The Love Bus travelled all over Europe in the mid 70s.
Belgian journalist Fata Morgana gets into the spirit of flower power.
Bessie – one of the original hippie buses.
Sergeant Pepper teaches the vans to play.

hard core of authentic alternative-culture followers. Known as Deadheads, these fans would faithfully follow the Grateful Dead on tour wherever they went, travelling from city to city and setting up camp as they travelled, living an alternative lifestyle on the road. One of their popular choices of vehicle was the VW bus. These decorated VW buses and wide-eyed, brightly dressed occupants are probably the origins of the hippie-bus stereotype.

By 1969, the Diggers (the original hippies) in San Francisco were upset at how the media were profiteering from hippie ideals. The Diggers wanted to make a statement that being a hippie was more than just a stereotype, or the way you looked and dressed – it was a way of living and being. To make this point, the Diggers devised a 'death of the hippie ceremony', marching down Haight Street with a coffin, while onlookers threw their love beads into the coffin. With the Hippie officially 'dead', the hip/peaceful people congregated around the Dead, i.e. the Grateful Dead, who were playing at the ceremony. As the band played, the Deadheads danced to mourn the passing of the hippie, with movements very similar to the Ghost Dance, the first intertribal religion of the Native Americans. Joseph Campbell, a world-renowned mythologist, called the Grateful Dead scene a cultural phenomenon similar to many ancient rituals, but unlike anything seen in modern times. Many of the Grateful Dead songs are actually old folk tales that tell stories going back hundreds of years.

Right: Rick Peters and Trudy Morgul were photographed atop the Light Bus at Woodstock (see also pages 98–99).

BESSIE: THE QUEEN OF LOVE

If any bus deserves the title of hippie bus, then it is this 1967 Sundial camper. She was discovered by Jacob Devaney in 1990 in the backyard of a bookstore in Farmville, Virginia. He was on his way to meet up with Ken Kesey and got chatting to the bus's owner, whose eyes lit up when he mentioned this. Apparently she had been one of the Pranksters and knew Ken well. She smiled and said, 'Let me show you something.' She then took Jacob into the backyard, and there was Bessie.

Bessie's owner had bought her fifteen years earlier when she lived in Eugene, Oregon, after many years spending time with the Merry Pranksters and the Grateful Dead. She had wanted to restore the bus but never found the time to get round to it, and when she offered to sell Bessie to Jacob he jumped at the chance. At that time Bessie was still in her original Pearl White paint and complete with her original Sundial seats, pull-out bed, water tank and sink, and wood panelling.

For the next five years Jacob toured in her following the Grateful Dead, until 1995 when Jerry Garcia, the driving force behind the band, died. It appeared that Bessie's glory days were over, when in stepped a group of 'Deadicated' artists and young people, some of whom were original Deadheads who had spent many years on tour with the Grateful Dead and were determined to keep the dream alive. They converged on Arizona and the legendary Mother Earth's Healing Circus was born. Bessie was to be the symbol of resurrection and, using paint found and reclaimed from skips, artist 'R' Wall designed the grand mural on her driver's side panel. Art Nouveau was given a 1960s psychedelic twist and combined with a Wild West 'Old Time Medicine Show' feel. The mural depicted a wizard, in the likeness of Jerry Garcia, waving a magic wand over the images. The scroll at the bottom read, 'Welcome to the Age of Living Folklore'.

On Easter Sunday 1996, with the reborn Bessie, they mounted an outdoor festival called The Resurrection of the Hippie, proclaiming:

'The Dance of the Dead has ended, and now it is time for a new generation to pick up the dance of the Living. This is a dance of healing; this is the age of the Mother Earth's Healing Circus and the Age of Living Folklore, where everybody lives the dream of peace left by our ancestors, the Dead.'

This led to the epic 'Love Is the Jester' two-year national tour, for which Bessie was crowned the Queen and lead vehicle. As Bessie entered each town, people hooted their horns, and curious onlookers, old and young, came out of the woodwork with stories of their own. Over the next three years she carted clowns, unicycles, stilts, assorted musical instruments and a trunk full of costumes and clown gags all over the United States. On one journey she drove from St Louis to Denver loaded with six circus performers, two unicycles, one bike, four pairs of stilts, a large box of costumes, a harp, a banjo, a saxophone, a clarinet, a fiddle, an electric piano and a two-year-old baby. Bessie's crowning glory came at her thirtieth birthday at the Oregon National Rainbow Gathering, where the Living Folklore Medicine Show performed the famous 'Clowns Take Over the Courtroom', with music provided by Spirit Union Revival.

Sadly, the time came when Bessie needed more attention than the clowns could give and she was reluctantly sold, to an uncertain future. Just one year later, she had been stripped and was literally fifteen minutes from being sold as scrap, when VW enthusiasts Jerry and Melissa Jess spotted her at the Jerome Jamboree show. They immediately recognised the unique nature of this bus and bought her. Determined to ensure that Bessie's story should be preserved, they set about getting her restored, including a refurbishment of murals by the artist Giggly Sprout. Now fully restored, with the interior kitted out with authentic period hippie regalia, Bessie continues to bring pleasure to people. Jacob sums up what Bessie symbolises:

Of course the hippie is a prankster, and you can't recognise one simply by the way they look, it is a way of being and acting with kindness. The hippie was DEAD (Gratefully) for twenty-six years and nobody knew it. Now the hippie has been resurrected, and guess who's gonna let the world know? We are! This whole thing with Bessie has really been a miracle, more than any of us could have dreamed, and it brings much joy. She was, and still is, a great Cinderella story, nothing stock! Now she is looking and running better than ever. Bessie remains a symbol of the strength within us all to create beauty and hope in the face of despair. Welcome to the Age of Living Folklore! Bessie has been at the death bed, only to return with a greater passion to awaken the dreamer within us all. As for the Living Folklore Clowns, well they always have a few jokers up their sleeve. If life is a story, make yours a good one... and you can always find us at www.livingfolklore.com.

LET LOVE RULE

It is surprising just how much interest a genuine hippie bus still gets from all corners of society. The 'Let Love Rule' bus is a case in point. This 1962 camper was found in Austria by Mark Walker of the Bus Station VW-bus business back in September 2003, while on a bus-buying tour of Europe. It had been owned during the mid-1970s by some freewheeling travellers, who still subscribed to the hippie ideals of the 60s and who were also responsible for its psychedelic paint job. They lived in their camper for several years, driving all over the Europe, attending festivals and chasing sunshine. By the close of the 70s the bus had changed hands, and it spent most of the next thirty years 'resting', before being discovered by Mark.

He brought it to England in time for Vanfest, where it sat for sale on the Bus Station trade stand. The camper attracted so many comments and photographs over the weekend that Mark often jokes, 'If we had charged a pound for each photo we would probably be able to retire.' He goes on to say, 'This has got to be the most talked-about van we have imported so far, with even Goodwood inviting us to the Revival with it last September!' Its paintwork is very rough and ready, but the van is a perfect example of the way a VW camper can express the lifestyle and individuality of its owners.

FLOWER POWER

Nostalgia for times gone by and fading dreams continues to capture the imagination of people everywhere. When the Belgian promoters of a special exhibition on the history of pop music were planning their event, they knew they wanted something iconic and eye-catching at the entrance. What better than a multicoloured VW camper to sum up the 1960s' explosion in youth culture and music? They contacted Bob Van Heyst, who runs BBT, a Belgian vintage-VW specialist company, who happened to have a rare 1954 Barndoor bus available. Bob had only recently acquired it and, after making it roadworthy, had put it into his famous vintage-VW museum collection, where it was awaiting a new paint job. He agreed to loan it to the promoters, provided they would paint the vehicle and return it to him in its psychedelic rebirth when the exhibition was finished.

Once the promoters had commissioned an artist to recreate the effect they were after, the bus was used as part of the entrance/ticket office to the exhibition to create just the right atmosphere for visitors, putting them in the mood to enjoy what they were about to experience. The exhibition in 2003 chronicled the history of pop, from the roots of blues through rock 'n' roll and acid rock, heavy metal, glam rock and punk into the modern day, and was so successful that it ran for two years. The bus is now back in Bob's private museum, and up for sale to anyone who wants to experience no-frills driving in the raw (a 1954 bus is very spartan and basic) – and who does not mind being the object of police attention wherever they go.

RE-LIVING THE DREAM IN A NEW MILLENNIUM

Of all the late-twentieth-century music festivals, the Glastonbury Festival is the one that has survived into the new millennium, and for many it is the epitome of what a music and alternative lifestyle festival is all about. The VW camper is an integral part of that, though one is more likely to see tidy, well-cared-for campervans than rough, tatty or psychedelic versions. With the unpredictable English weather, a camper also offers refuge from the sheets of rain and seas of mud that so often make Glastonbury a unique experience. For some campervan owners, taking the VW to Glastonbury is a rite of passage; for others it is almost a pilgrimage. Music, the open air, green fields, happy shiny people, colour, vibrancy and the chance to meet up with like-minded people seeking escape from humdrum reality – the low-tech lifestyle of living with a VW bus is the only way to get into what Glastonbury is all about.

THE HIPPIES ARE BACK

Although there remain only a tiny number of travellers who try to live life simply and in harmony with nature, the association of hippies, happy days and hope with the VW bus is still paid homage to at VW bus gatherings. Apart from anything else, it's great fun to dress up in bizarre and colourful clothes (usually now only seen in embarrassing photos of one's parents when young). Events like VW Action have even themed their whole weekend around flower power, with retro acts in the dance tents to recreate the atmosphere. In 2005, Vanfest, the biggest bus festival on the planet, saw a huge gathering of fancy-dress 'hippies' of all ages (although a breakaway faction came as Punks) bopping the night away to classic Cream and Pink Floyd tracks. There was even a marriage proposal live on stage. One wonders what the original hippies would make of all this – but it's likely they would smile, say, 'Far out, man' and get stuck into the vibe.

MAKING THE WORLD A BETTER PLACE

While the ideals of the 1960s may be fading and tarnished, for some campervan owners their vehicle is a way to keep those dreams alive by bringing joy and practical aid to the less fortunate in society. Of the many uses the VW bus is put to, raising money for charity is one way that thoughtful and caring owners can give something back to the world. The unique nature of the VW bus means that it always gets noticed and smiled at, and it is versatile enough to be able to carry people and aid and even advertise what is going on. In the UK, VW campers have raised money for charities like Children In Need, with buses touring the country and stopping to fund-raise in towns and villages en route. Decorated campers festooned with balloons join in carnival parades in many towns, collecting money for local charities from onlookers. The three examples described here, from the UK, Germany and the United States, give a flavour of the many different ways people today work and live with their campers to help others.

THE GUTHRIE WALK

The heritage of the VW camper's central role in the movie *Alice's Restaurant* (see page 78) has resulted in an annual fund-raising event for Huntingdon's Disease called 'the Guthrie Walk.' Woody Guthrie (Arlo's father) was seen in hospital in the movie and later died from Huntingdon's Disease. As a direct result of this tragic event, the family set up a centre for research into this debilitating disease; a recent spin-off has been to use VW campers to support and ferry walkers, who raise money from sponsorship. Lisa Guthrie, married to one of Woody's grandchildren, handles much of the publicity for the event and recounts how it all came about:

In the summer of 2000 a group of HD [Huntingdon's Disease] folks came to the Guthrie Center from the Laurel Lake Center HD Program in Lee, Massachusetts, for a day of exercise, lunch and just to hang out, when one of the women with HD said, 'I wish someone would do a walk for us.' So Jim Pollard from the Center and I started thinking maybe we could do Arlo's 'Historic Garbage Trail'. Not knowing how long it was, we drove it a couple times and realised it was a little over six miles – do-able! So that winter we started planning it. We decided on May, because it is National Huntingdon's Disease Month. VW Microbuses just made sense for rides for everyone back to the Center (which is the church made famous in *Alice's Restaurant*) as it was in one of those that Arlo got busted. We went to our local VW dealer in Pittsfield, and talked with Jim D. there, who owns an old Microbus himself. He set us up with some drivers, we sent out the walk info to the Guthrie Center members and the HD families, and the rest is history.

The walk begins at the 'church' and goes through the town of Housatonic, and into Stockbridge, via the 'town dump' and the 'police officer's station', where we warmly remember Officer Obie and get our pictures taken behind the door of the cell that held Arlo, before heading on down to the former Alice's Restaurant, which is now Theresa's. There, everyone has sandwiches, drinks and Theresa's famous chocolate chip cookies! Then everyone piles into the old Microbuses for their ride back to the 'church'. The first year [2001] we raised about six thousand dollars for the care and cure of HD with about seventy-something walkers, and by 2003 we were raising over twenty thousand dollars with about two hundred walkers! For us, it has been awesome to watch this walk grow and hear everyone looking forward to it each year.

All the money raised is divided equally between Casa Hogar, a community in Venezuela with over 1,000 people living with Huntingdon's Disease, and the Marjorie Guthrie Fund, which is the international HD group. This money helps with getting HD information typed up in different languages and getting people from other countries to conferences to learn the latest information on the disease.

In the original movie *Alice's Restaurant* the VW bus symbolised fun, freedom and hope, and it's good to see that, nearly forty years on, the VW bus is now being used to help people find freedom and hope for the future. You can find out more about Casa Hogar and the Marjorie Guthrie Fund by emailing Jim Pollard, the HD guru to families living with this disease, on jjpollard@comcast.net.

In keeping with the spirit of the original film, VW Campers are used to ferry walkers back and a carnival atmosphere uplifts everyone.

MUSTARD SEED MINISTRIES

From April to October every year a brightly painted VW camper carries 2.5 tons of trade stands and goods to festivals and VW shows all over England and Wales. The Little India stall, run by the husband-and-wife team Papa Rick and Gilly, sells clothes, fabrics and handicrafts, and all money raised goes directly to support their charity, Mustard Seed Ministries. They set this up in 1993 to support and help street children and orphans in India, as a direct result of seeing at first hand the appalling poverty and lack of a future facing many of these children. After visiting Goa as a tourist, Rick began to feel that something should be done to help the children begging on the beaches, and then finally realised that the 'something' was down to him.

Their first efforts involved setting up a school on the beach under an old parachute. As well as feeding the children and providing some basic education, they also helped the children learn to stay away from certain types of predatory adult tourist. At one Christmas party they fed and gave presents to over 180 children.

Their involvement since those early days has resulted in them now supporting several refuges and homes set up to help children who are orphans, are from dysfunctional families, are emotionally damaged or have special needs. Mustard Seed Ministries does not own or run the projects but aims to provide finance, support and encouragement for local people who have heart and vision. Recently they have become involved with Faith and Football,

Rick and Gilly with Pedro and Gemilda Lima, House Parents from the Shallom House in Goa, with some of the crafts they sell to raise money for their charity work.

which is based in Portsmouth, and which is now actively supporting and fund-raising for the building of a church, orphanage, care home, medical centre and housing in Goa.

As well as being actively hands-on when they are in India, for example project-managing building work, Rick and Gilly also use the time to source local crafts and products. These are then brought back to England and sold to raise money. They buy directly from families and build up relationships with them, which in turn helps the local economy. Despite five heart attacks and a quadruple-bypass operation, Papa Rick is still going strong and attributes this to his Christian faith.

VW campers have always been part of Rick's life, and two buses are currently being restored by a local mechanic in Goa for use in their work out there. The Little India bus is used every weekend to take the Little India stall and wares out on the road and, with its brightly coloured paintwork, gets a lot of notice and always makes people smile.

If you would like to help support Rick and Gilly's work, they can be contacted on streetkids@msm.org.uk.

BULLIS BRINGEN FREUDE

Michael Steinke admits to being a VW-bus obsessive and is widely respected in the bus world for his expertise and knowledge. Formerly one of the guiding lights of Bulli Kartei, the German Split Bus Club, he now runs the Westfalia Register and has written many books on the history and uses of the VW bus, in all its forms and generations. He is also someone who cares passionately about the world we live in.

Back in 1992, Michael and a few like-minded friends began to find the usual VW shows and camping weekends rather samey. The war in Bosnia was in the headlines, and images of ravaged countryside, bombed-out towns, and desperate families caught up in something beyond their control were on everyone's TV screens. What was even more disturbing was that this was taking place in Europe, right on their doorstep. As they sat around their campers one evening, talk turned to the plight of innocent people and how they could help. Remembering slogans from old VW adverts for emergency and utility models like 'the VW Transporter – your helper in danger and need', the group began to wonder how they could use some of these now decommissioned VWs to help those facing danger and need. The idea of creating an aid convoy using old VW buses and campers was born: Bullis Bringen Freude, which translates as 'buses bring joy', was about to become a reality.

Since then BBF has undertaken twenty-four missions to Bosnia and Romania, taking medicines, clothes, toys, tools, kitchenware, heaters and bikes to orphanages and care centres. Vehicles used include modern T4s and old Split campers, panel vans, pickups and double cabs, ambulances and a high-roof bus full of spares. Latterly, as stability began to return to the areas, equipment for the disabled such as wheelchairs and bath hoists began to make up the bulk of the aid. BBF has even donated old VW ambulances and pickup trucks to organisations. Items are sourced through donations, and money is raised through garage sales, bazaars and raffles. One major source of funds comes from the sale of specially commissioned Brekina models of campers and buses used in the convoys. Not only are these highly sought after by collectors, but they are also an easy way for any VW-bus fan to make a contribution.

As peace returned and governments began to create some order, the convoys fell foul of levies from transit countries and also import duties – so much so that by 2003 it was becoming too costly to continue the humanitarian convoys. Therefore, in 2004 the group decided to do something a little different, and combine a holiday with a BBF fund-raising tour. This time they came to Britain, and a friend in Scotland suggested they could donate money to the Daisy Chain Trust, which works to raise money for research into, and treatment of, breast cancer. A specially commissioned Brekina model of the high-roof support bus was chosen to raise funds for the charity, and it sold very well. The group were able to meet up with friends and bus lovers in England and Scotland, and present a cheque to Lady Kirkwood, who chairs the Daisy Chain Trust, before heading off for a holiday in the Scottish Highlands.

Combining a passion for old campers with a desire to spread some happiness and help others is what BBF is all about. As Buddha said, 'Even by the falling of drops a water pot is filled.' Michael jokes that BBF now means many things, 'Buses Bring Funds… Friendship… Fun.

People and their campers can, and do, make a difference. Some dreams are still being kept alive.

7 PAINT YOUR VOLKSWAGEN!

The large sides of a VW bus have always presented the perfect blank canvas for individuals to express themselves on. The very first Transporter to roll off the production line back in March 1950 was delivered, in factory primer, to the 4711 perfume company, which promptly painted it in its own colours and livery – the ideal mobile billboard. Other companies followed suit and by the 1960s Volkswagen even produced an advertising brochure showing liveried buses in use all over the world, in order to promote the idea to businesses and fire their imaginations to the possibilities.

The standard VW colours were pastel shades, and only the Microbuses were finished in two-tone as standard. By 1958 the dark-over-light scheme had been replaced with light-over-dark, with pale greys and whites used for the top half. Body colours were pastel shades of red, green, blue and grey, designed to blend in rather than shout. The multi-purpose Kombi models were single-colour, with grey blue, pale grey and ivory white being the most common shades. Camper conversions stayed with standard VW colours and it was not until the 1970s that oranges, bright blues and deep reds came into the range. Metallics had to wait until 1980.

By the late 60s, however, buses were being owned and driven by a new generation. Inspired by the psychedelia explosion and the hippie movement, young people saw the perfect opportunity to express themselves and their culture by personalising their cheap, reliable (and usually tatty) campers in wild and wacky ways. Partly they wanted to express their own values and show the world they were different and that the standard camper pastels of their parents had to go, but it was also a cheap and easy way to cover rust and tired paint. What's more, a fun and creative 'paint the bus party' was much more satisfying than painting walls in a friend's dingy basement flat. Some campers, however, are more than just a fun mishmash of colour and are works of art in their own right.

Seen at the Beach Buggin Show in Poole, this camper is always in sun-drenched paradise.

A BUS CALLED LIGHT

During the 1960s, many bands and musicians used VW campers and buses to tour in. As well as being cheap to buy and run, they had character and could haul lots of gear. One such band was Light, hailing from Baltimore, Maryland. Their bus was painted by the Baltimore artist Dr Bob Hieronimus in 1968 and the next year was photographed at Woodstock with two band members sitting on the roof enjoying the vibe (see page 79). The photo was used in most newspapers and magazines of the time, from the *New York Times* to *Rolling Stone* magazine, and has become a seminal image, capturing the spirit of the event and of the time. It also inspired a whole new look for the VW camper.

It was when the musician Bob Grimm saw his friend Dr Bob's artwork on his own Beetle, called 'Old Smoke', that Grimm asked Dr Bob to paint a mural on his VW bus, which his band used for hauling gear to gigs. Contrary to media myth, the bus was not painted specifically to go to Woodstock and, although often described as 'the Woodstock bus', it was actually called Light, after the name of the band. Dr Bob had already painted a few vehicles and had just been commissioned to create a mural for a meeting room at Johns Hopkins University.

Dr Bob was very into 'esoteric art', which drew on ageless wisdom and teachings from classic cultures and mythology. He viewed the painting of vehicles as a way of creating mobile 'billboards' that communicated ideas about the nature of existence and man's place in the universal scheme of things. In addition, Dr Bob saw the possibilities the shape of the VW offered, in that a design could be wrapped round the sides and roof, allowing for greater detail and continuity of theme.

Top: Bob Grimm with the Light bus and Dr Bob's Beetle.

Below: The murals tell a story of advanced beings helping humankind achieve cosmic consciousness.

As well as creating murals, Dr Bob also spent most of the summer of 1968 hanging out backstage with artists such as Jimi Hendrix, the Doors and Peter Rowan's Earth Opera, discussing astrology, Atlantis, reincarnation, meditation and UFOs. However, he soon tired of the exhausting lifestyle of travel, where he had no art studio and was constantly on the move with just his satchel and sketchbook, so he was grateful to return to Baltimore where he could be at peace creating art. Bob Grimm got excited about the idea of these themes being painted on his bus, and so, before starting work on his mural project for the university, Dr Bob set about completing the Light bus. The bus was designed to take the band to gigs and get noticed wherever they were playing, which it certainly did.

Despite having a ticket, Bob missed going to Woodstock as he was immersed in his work, but Bob Grimm and members of Light – Rick Peters, Walt Bailey and Trudy Morgul – went, taking the Light bus. Because of the dreadful mud they drove it to higher ground and spent much of the time on the roof of the bus, enjoying the vibe and listening to Santana, Jefferson Airplane, Arlo Guthrie, Hendrix, The Who, Country Joe, and Crosby Stills and Nash, to name just a few of the rock legends who played at the event. It was Rick and Trudy who were photographed atop the bus and who were to become the anonymous symbols of the Woodstock generation.

Unlike the stereotypical hippie bus, the design was meticulously planned and executed so that all the symbols, scripts and designs worked in harmony, with the two sides and front coming together at both an aesthetic and a symbolic level. The story shown tells of advanced beings in the universe, in various dimensions, who are enabling and assisting our awareness and evolution to cosmic consciousness. The front panel shows that as we enter the Age of

Aquarius we will once more become conscious of what has gone before and where we are going. The Eagle panel (left side) depicts America's destiny to bring together all the people of the Earth. The Sphinx panel (loading-door side) represents all the various influences that are working and have worked to assist in the fulfilment of this destiny for humankind. Dr Bob later said:

'With hindsight it is interesting that the symbols I painted on this bus were very much in harmony with this powerful event [Woodstock]. Those with eyes to see and ears to hear realised that it carried the message of who we are and the purpose of life on Planet Earth: serving others as we evolve toward cosmic consciousness.'

For those wishing to discover more about how to interpret the Light bus, Dr Bob has explained in detail the symbols and meanings on his website, www.21stcenturyradio.com/woodstockbus.htm, where you can also see more of his artwork and murals.

Not only was Light one of the first VW campers to be painted in this way, but its Woodstock heritage adds to its importance and influence on the future. It is not just another 'hippie bus', but a work of art in its own right which captures the mood and aspirations of a generation searching for its own identity and place in the universal scheme of things. The bus may have passed into legend, but its legacy as inspiration for new generations of camper owners lives on.

Currently, Dr Bob is working on another painted car, his first in over ten years. It's a 1983 Mercedes sedan he has named 'Dark Horse', which he is painting with themes from his book *Founding Fathers and Secret Societies*, available from Inner Traditions International in 2006.

THE SPIRIT OF SALCOMBE

The tradition of brightly coloured, so-called hippie buses, sporting flowers, astrological symbols and psychedelic patterns, was mainly seen in the United States. It captured the freewheeling spirit of the times so much that this image is now linked with the VW bus in the minds of many; but times have changed, and there are also still campers that are works of art in their own right, albeit in a very different way from the Light bus. A good example is Fred Crellin's 1972 camper, which takes a naturalistic approach to camper art with its fantastically detailed airbrushed views of the Salcombe coast in Devon adorning all its sides.

Known as The Spirit of Salcombe, or Sally for short, it was bought by Fred Crellin in September 2002, when it had ropey yellow and white paintwork. As well as teaching design technology part-time, Fred also runs Artimagination Airbrushing and the Artimagination Airbrush School, and so airbrushing the bus all over was the logical way to go. Fred is passionate about surfing and especially loves the Salcombe coastline, so he took this as the inspiration for the design, using photographs of the coastline he had taken himself as the starting point. The airbrushing was all done by Fred and took him four months to complete, including working through

the day and night over Christmas and New Year. Fred explains what he likes best about driving Sally:

'It always gives me such a buzz to see the delight on people's faces who see her for the first time... especially on long motorway journeys... somehow, I get the feeling most of them know where we're going or where we've been... I can't think how!'

Sally even served as the bride's transport for Fred and Ginny's wedding, and she continues to draw crowds and admiring looks wherever she travels, though Fred does get upset by people who ask him if it's a sticker.

TIGER BAY

Tony and Yvonne Sulley are hard-core veedubbers. As well as helping set up and run the Born Again VeeDub Club, they spend most weekends away in their camper, either at a show or with fellow club members. The club's not one of those 'rules and committees' affairs, but more like one large extended family, which meets up for a big family do every weekend.

Tony and Yvonne came up with the idea of a Dub Safari Bus as a way of doing something different with an orange and white camper. Tony immediately set about doing the interior in leopard print, while Yvonne began to collect accessories round the theme, from crockery to cuddly toys. Yvonne's uncle is a signwriter and coach painter by trade and, after much persuasion, agreed to paint the bus for them. Using coachwork enamel, all the tiger striping and blending was done by hand and eye in the garage, with access to only one side at a time. The result is stunning and only cost about fifty pounds. Their Beetle, also seen here, was originally painted to match but, since their son Joe took possession, it has been transformed into a very different guise.

RASPBERRY SPLIT

Flames have long been associated with hot rods and custom cars, and the tradition is well represented in the VW camper world. Mike and Kate Port have owned this camper since 2001. Called Raspberry Split (the name coming from its colour and model), the camper had originally been a Swedish blue and white Microbus, which at some point had been repainted red and white and fitted with a craftsman-built interior. It had come with front safaris, five-spoke Empi wheels, a new Vege engine and a recon gearbox, and all Mike had to do initially was to overhaul all the brakes before setting about creating the look he wanted.

After a lowering job, Mike followed the American Hot Rod street-style look, applying black and white checking to the beltline and front panel V shape, wing mirrors, wheel centre caps, inside the headlights and on the dash, and fitting checked mudflaps. Beauty rings were fitted to the wheels and Redline striping to the tyres, while Kate refurbished the interior using Salt Rock fabric with a white leatherette centre section on the interior panels. An eight-ball gear knob, tinted windows and aluminium silver pinstriping round the safaris rounded off the look. The arrival of baby Josie spurred some interior modifications like the making of a 'door gate' (to fit between the seats, creating a safe playpen).

In 2003, when the paintwork started to bubble around the door and wheel-arch areas, necessitating cutting out the rot and replacing the front valence and nearside wheel arch, Mike had the ideal opportunity to go for the full Hot Rod Flame look he had always wanted. By matching the flames to incorporate the

repaired areas he was able to repaint these portions and at the same time achieve a new look. Mike designed the shapes and look using fine-line masking tape, while his friend Ant applied the paint with Mike watching and advising as the pattern took shape. The result is stunning, making the bus into a real head-turner – so much so that the *Sunday Times* featured the bus in their write-up about the 2004 Run to the Sun event.

The camper is also detailed with many individual and personal arty touches, including the gecko crawling up the roof, the aerial ball, stencilling on the roof cupboard, and even an optic drinks bottle. Mike is constantly working on adding detail touches to the bus – even while they are using it. A hibiscus flower pattern on the dash, for example, was stencilled during one of their surfing weekends, after Mike had spotted the stencils for sale in a local shop.

Surfing, camping and VW buses are what this family is all about, and they can't imagine life without all three. The camper is perfect for their impetuous and free-spirited lifestyle and is always kitted out with everything, including food and bedding, so they can literally go anywhere, anytime, at a moment's notice. The interior is totally child-friendly and, despite Josie's arrival, most weekends are still spent at either Woolacombe or Croyde, checking out the surf. Josie already has her own wetsuit and adores being in the bus, whether using her own steering wheel when riding up front with her dad or playing in her own 'room'. Surf's up – break out the boards!

THE GOTH BUS

This T25 started life as a humble panel van back in 1986. After two years of lugging stuff around, it ended up in Bristol Car Auctions. Mike Goldsmith had just been made redundant and was looking for something cheap and reliable, and preferably VW, and this 1600 diesel van fitted the bill (and his pocket) perfectly. A panel van presented the perfect blank canvas for Mike to work on. He fitted a Leisuredrive Interior Kit, side windows and an elevating roof, and the panel van was transformed into a comfy camper. A shiny new red paint job and bright side decals were complemented with a new number plate, VUW 666 – and the Red Devil was ready to rock and roll and steal some souls. The mark of the beast was such that at weekends Mike sported a special matching polo shirt with 'Red Devil' emblazoned on it.

In 2004, someone swiped the entire side in Sainsbury's car park (and drove off), meaning that the new paint job Mike had been promising himself became a necessity. He finally found exactly the shade of red he was looking for – Mazda MX5 metallic red, which has an orange or gold sheen when the light catches it.

Mike had quite liked the original decals but he decided this time round to go for something wild and different, and decided to 'Goth it up' with airbrushed panels. He came up with the idea of a dragon across the whole roof that looked like it was swooping when the roof was up, and had ideas about undead and spectres, but in the end he handed over complete design responsibility to Mal Roberts, whose original artwork is well known in the biker community. Artwork was hand-drawn onto acetate and then projected onto the areas to be airbrushed. Mike could hardly believe the transformation when he saw the finished result, and he says he feels he's King of the Road while driving it. He also loves the fact it's no bigger than a modern car but offers so much versatility, meaning he can stop whenever and wherever he wants to. Oh, and he loves disturbing people's psyches, too. The Goths are back in town… lock up your children!

T25 RETRO TWIST

Lol and Rob Cracknell have only recently got into the world of VW campers. After having been serious tenters for years, they fancied the idea of arriving somewhere with everything all ready. So, just before Vanfest 2005, they bought a T25 camper and let their daughter Rachel and her college friend Louise loose on it to 'brighten her up'. Using spray cans and stencils, the girls did all the work in just two days. Rob and Rachel proudly show off the results in the photograph shown above.

The resulting mix of flower-power retro and modern urban styles was a major talking point at the show, and Rob and Lol were surprised at the interest shown in 'Molly' and at the way they were instantly taken into the VW bus 'family' – so much so, that by the end of the weekend they had made many new friends. They are now looking forward to getting into the bus scene, as well as using their camper for weekends away. Rob loves the look Rachel has created for the bus, saying, 'You'll always know it's us coming!'

TWO SIDES TO EVERY STORY

This owner was spotted in the act of painting his camper in his driveway in Devon. He saw it as a way of brightening the bus and using up all the old tins of paint in his garage, and he found nothing strange about a family on holiday pulling up to chat about his bus and take some pictures.

GALLERY

For VW camper owners, personalising a camper is an important ritual, and the way you paint your bus is a key part of that. While some opt for the totally stock route, using the original colours from the period, others go for bright modern colours and metallics. Conversely, there are those who buck the trend for shiny restored campers, opting instead for the 'Rat Look' (see page 17), in which rust, primer and faded paintwork are *de rigueur*. Deciding which colours to choose, and what will go with what, can sometimes take many months. People have been known to go to the Paint Shop saying, 'Can you match this bath towel/cuddly toy/dress?' There is even a website where you can play around with different colour combinations.

Perhaps, in part, it's the heritage of the brightly painted gypsy caravan that lives on in the consciousness of those who live their life with a VW camper – after all, it was Devon campers who in the 1960s coined the slogan 'Be as free as a Gypsy in a Devon Caravette'.

The campers shown here are just a tiny sample of the many and varied ways it is possible to Paint Your Volkswagen.

Deciding what colour to paint your camper is nothing compared with deciding how the interior should be finished! The camper's interior is living room, lounge, dining room, kitchen, bedroom and even children's playroom. It needs to be somewhere to relax but also has to be functional. In addition, it may need to double as a people-carrier, school-run minibus or even load-lugger. The versatility of a camper means it can be used for any job, from moving house to taking rubbish to the dump or carrying the winter's supply of logs.

The various professional camping conversions have covered every conceivable layout and design to fit cooking, washing, dining, seating and sleeping arrangements into a tiny space. Apart from the traditional dinette, there are L-shaped seating arrangements, seats that can face backwards or forwards, door-mounted fold-down cookers, kitchens arranged down one side or in the rear – the possibilities and varieties seem limitless.

Even so, there are still those who need or want to design an interior to suit their own lifestyle, adding serious sound systems, DVD-players or even cocktail cabinets. And, as in any home, as well as the furniture there are the curtains, fabrics and flooring to be chosen – interior design is a serious business. As can be seen in the camper interiors depicted in this chapter, camping is also about style and taste as well as functionality.

In keeping with exterior styling, there are several routes – stock/period, custom and designer – although there is still a place for the 'rough-and-ready chuck in the sleeping bags and crates of beer' interior. While modern campers now boast showers, microwaves and a degree of luxury not found in most people's homes, there is often a certain blandness about them. A classic VW camper, however, retains charm and individuality. For the owners it is their home, and they make it such. Every camper is different, because the owners are different. Owners bring something of themselves to their bus. Whether in its furnishings, accessories, modifications or colour schemes, their camper is an extension of their personality, their values, their creativity, their lifestyle.

Previous pages, from left to right:

Traditional Dormobile seats have been re-trimmed and matching side panels fitted.

A small circular table creates more space.

Original period Westfalia interior from 1963.

Draught beer and optics mean this owner always has the pub with him!

Sweeping curves and a light grain wood give an airy, modern look.

Right: Meditation chamber.

Opposite: New upholstery and curtains can transform a tired interior.

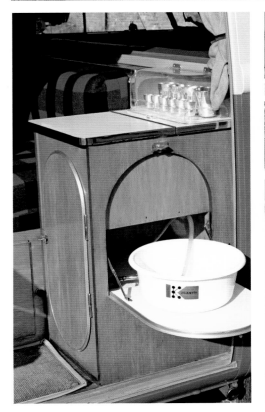

STOCK INTERIORS

For some owners, a fully original interior (or a faithful copy of one) is the only conceivable route. They see campers as living history, things of beauty to be preserved and enjoyed by generations to come. Although completely original and hardly used campers still turn up, it usually takes months of research and hunting on the internet or at shows to source those missing pieces that will return the camper to how it would have been when it was first sold. While not everyone wants to own a piece of living history (or to have the responsibility of keeping it like that to pass on), everyone loves and appreciates an original, period interior.

To hard-core camper enthusiasts, the 1959 Westfalia conversion, designated SO 23, is the Holy Grail of campers. It has many beautiful distinctive features, which set the trend for others to follow. These prized features include wood panelling throughout, red and black check fabrics, birchwood cabinets, clamshell-design light shades and the first-ever cocktail cabinet to be fitted in a camper, complete with spun-aluminium tumblers. There is even a cargo net hung in the rear for shoes and such-like. In the camper shown here all the period features remain intact, all the awning and poles are complete and there is even an original bucket toilet.

The camper had been bought from new in 1960 by two sisters, who ordered it direct from the factory before flying out from the United States to collect it. Having just retired, they spent the next six months touring Europe, living in the camper, before shipping the vehicle back to New York and then driving it across the whole of the United States back home to California. Amazingly they duplicated the entire trip four years later, in 1964. They used the camper all the time, until 1977 when, after one sister died, it was put into a large shed. It remained there undisturbed for the next twenty years, before it was eventually uncovered by a nephew in 1997.

The camper caused a storm when it debuted at a show in that year, having been rescued, cleaned, polished and tuned. It then passed through the hands of two serious collectors, before being snapped up by UK resident Tony Best when it came up for sale on the internet. It is probably one of the finest unrestored, original condition examples of an early camper to still grace the roads instead of residing in a museum. Although the camper now wins awards and is the centre of attention wherever it goes, Tony and his family enjoy using it for exactly what it was originally designed for – family holidays and camping.

PERSONAL DESIGNS

Other owners look at their conversion with an eye to how it can be improved and adapted to their own needs. Often they will rip out what is there (especially if it is not complete or is a hotchpotch) and start from scratch to design and build their own interior, taking inspiration from conversions seen at shows. Interiors are a constant source of fascination, and people trawl shows for ideas – and not just on the show and shine field. Ask any bus owner to show you their interior and you have a new friend for life.

When Mike Howles bought his 1972 Devon camper, the original fittings and furniture were so beaten up that restoration was not worth the effort. Mike and his wife Diane enjoy walking and love using the camper to get out into the countryside. They also love the crafted wood Devon interiors, which by 1972 had been replaced by melamine and laminate. Being a bit of a woodwork enthusiast, Mike felt he could create an interior that would better suit their needs. This meant the interior had to be built in wood and resemble the classic early Devon designs. On top of this, it had to suit their outdoor lifestyle while at the same time being practical and easy to use.

The bed space had to allow some floor area for keeping boots and gear handy, as well as allowing space to put the boots on without having to fold away the bed. The interior had to convert from day to night use with the minimum of fuss, and be able to seat four round a table when required. In addition, the cooker and sink had to be easily accessible from the bed to make that early morning cup of tea without having to get up. A fridge was an essential item (warm wine just doesn't cut it) – and the walkthrough cab feature had to be retained.

With ingenious and meticulous planning, what Mike has designed and crafted does all this, allowing seating for two or four, plenty of floor space and ample storage. The end result is a very individual interior that is subtly different from production models. To carry the look into the cab area, Mike added more woodwork in the form of an under-dash parcel tray, handbrake handle, gear knob and CD-player shelf for a personal CD-player. Based on classic design, with subtle changes to suit their own lifestyle, the overall look retains all the period feel of a 1960s interior, underlined by its emphasis on wood.

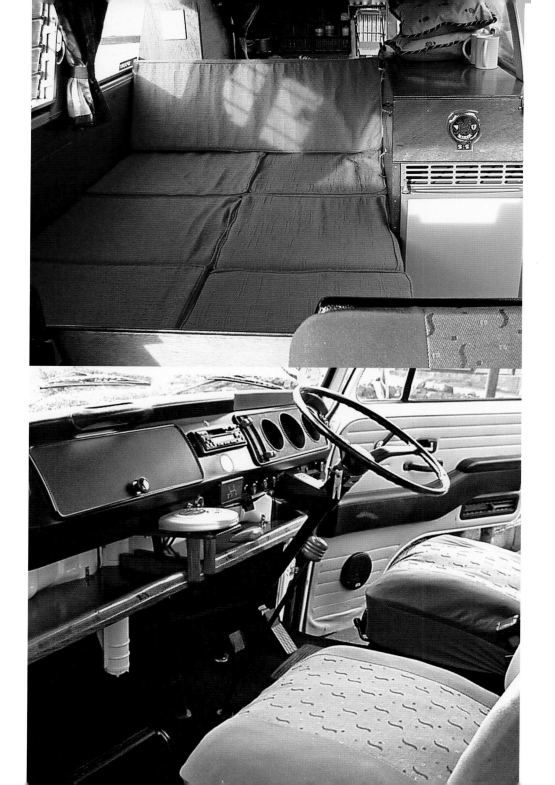

A MODERN CLASSIC

The 1964 camper pictured here was bought over the internet by Justin Coyne, and, as it had a tatty custom camping interior, he decided to start afresh. Taking inspiration from early Westfalias, especially the birch panelling throughout, and from interiors he had seen at shows, he set about planning the design on his laptop. He wanted to keep a period feel to the vehicle while creating a stylish, designer-look interior, which would be both practical and modern.

After repainting the camper in its original 1964 colours of Turkis Green (turquoise) and Blue White, the starting point inside was simply to be able to seat four in the back and have a table to sit at. In order to be practical to use for camping, there also had to be sufficient storage space and an easy-to-lay-out 'rock-and-roll' (pull-out) bed. Using light-oak ply, he made new door and side panels and a matching roof liner, following the Westfalia look. Furniture was also finished in matching light oak, and the upholstery then trimmed in cream leatherette, with green piping and trim in the precise shade of green to match the body colour. The harmonising check curtain fabric and fitted cream woollen carpets throughout finish the look. The attention to detail that is a hallmark of this camper can be seen in the overlocking at the edges of all the carpets.

A matching wood table is hinged to flap down against the side wall, another early Westy design feature. To divide the cab from the rear and hide the somewhat messy end of the front vent, another piece of shaped oak was fitted, mirroring the overhead cupboard door at the rear of the bus. The modern-looking sink is actually a stainless steel dog bowl, but would look classy in any bathroom, and a cool minimalist-style single-burner gas ring provides cooking facilities. A CD stereo is discreetly fitted behind the driver's seat; one pair of speakers with handmade surrounds is sited in the cab and another pair is located in the rear cupboards. There is also a separate split charging system for the leisure battery, to power the stereo when parked up and chilling!

The overall effect is a classic camper with a very modern twist. The spacious, airy, light interior features classic design elements, updated to reflect the needs and tastes of a new generation.

CUSTOM INTERIORS

Finally, there are those who set out to create something to subvert preconceived ideas of a VW-camper interior. These people conceptualise something different from the norm, and interior design is integral to the look they want to create. They are at the cutting edge, pushing back the boundaries as to what it is possible to do with a VW bus and its interior.

Simon Kerr's camper illustrates this perfectly. He has transformed his tatty, tired camper into something that is totally unique. His starting point was to design something that fitted his lifestyle and, after toying with all the different combinations of where to site the sink, cooker and bed, he realised that really all he wanted was somewhere to relax with friends in comfort. Space was what was important for this, and the only 'camping' requisite was a bed, since cooking and washing could easily be done outside or under an awning. He decided that the best way to achieve this was to have L-shaped seating, with no clutter

or table in the middle. The side bench has been designed to convert quickly and easily into a comfortable and roomy bed, which still allows standing room at the side by the door.

Having already decided on the brown and cream colour scheme for the outside (Simon was inspired by seeing the camper under orange street lighting), it seemed natural to carry the scheme right through the interior. The hibiscus flower design airbrushed onto the roof was a custom touch harking back to surfing and Hawaiian shirts, and this too has been carried into the interior, creating a harmonised look that links the exterior and interior. Simon wanted to restrict the colour scheme to brown, beige and cream and all the panels, carpets, interior paint and upholstery echo this theme. Finishing touches like the cream detailing on the seats and the sisal matting add to the overall harmonious look. The cab area is colour-coded to match, and the clever addition of a swivelling front seat means everyone can relax together.

The new sunroof not only lets in lots of natural light and warmth in summer but also means Simon and his mates can sit under the stars while putting the world to rights. (However, Simon says that cutting a seven-foot hole in the metal roof was very scary.) Soft lighting is achieved by downlighters inset in the roof walls below the sunroof and uplighters in the footwells. A hot/cold unit, with the door painted to match the exterior colour, means Simon can keep his pie and chips warm on the way back to the campsite or have an endless supply of cold beer. At the rear is a glass-topped storage area, which acts as a tabletop for glasses and bottles.

No home is complete without a sound system, and once again Simon showed imagination. Speakers have been mounted into swivel lamps in the rear, allowing music to come from different directions or to blast out through the doors, and there is a twelve-inch sub woofer under the rear seat and three-and-a-half-inch speakers in the cab. Simon describes the combined sound output of this set-up as 'ear bleeding'.

RED STRIPE

The Red Stripe bus is another example of exterior and interior design working in harmony. Using the colours and logos of this famous brand of Jamaican beer, the exterior paint matches the brand's red and white, with chrome trim for the silver detailing. While the outside has a subtle look, the interior is quite radical. The red and white theme continues, with panelling in red and white stripes and upholstery in red, with white roll edges. The most distinctive and talked-about touch, however, is the use of a surfboard, painted in Red Stripe colours and logo, for the central table. This bus has already been an inspiration for others, and interiors like this show what is possible with a bit of imagination.

GALLERY

New upholstery, flooring and curtains in bright modern fabrics and colours, can transform a tired or tatty interior and offer an easy way to update an old-fashioned look. The ubiquitous orange, brown and beige fabrics, in swirling colours or flower patterns, are probably best left in the 1970s where they belong. The interiors shown in the gallery illustrate just some of the endless possibilities and variety of ways in which camper interiors can be personalised to suit the tastes and lifestyles of their owners. Whether old jeans or modern Burberry, it's all about style.

9 ANTIPODEAN ADVENTURES

The attraction of sun, surf and a laid-back lifestyle, plus the chance to travel in some remote, beautiful and untouched wilderness in an Aussie Kombi Camper, is something that has long been known to young Brits in search of adventure, and old Kombis can still be bought relatively cheaply down under. Danger and excitement come from pitting oneself against nature rather than people, and exploring in the Outback also offers the chance to get off the beaten track without the fear of political turmoil erupting around you.

Previous pages, from left to right:

Wild camping on Grove Peninsula Beach, northern Australia.

Cactus Point surf spot is 200 miles from the nearest town.

Camping in the outback with Desert Splitty.

The Desert Splitty tackling rough terrain in Airhelmland, Northern Territory.

Right and opposite: A group of Aussie bus freaks taking on the Simpson desert in south-west Queensland, one of the biggest sand ridge deserts in the world.

The VW camper scene in Australia is somewhat different from anywhere else. For a start all buses are known as Kombis to Aussies, regardless of model or interior fitments. The Kombi has a reputation for being a cheap, practical vehicle, and certainly not something that has thousands of pounds lavished on it and then is displayed on a show field! Then of course comes the fact that unlike the UK, where old buses rust and need endless attention to beat the tinworm, the Australian climate means the vehicles go on, and on, and on. In fact Australia is now one of the fastest growing sources of rust-free buses, and imports to the UK are rising dramatically to meet the seemingly insatiable demand for reasonably priced, solid buses, which have the added bonus of being right-hand drive, unlike imports from the US and Europe. VW Australia built VWs in their own factory, using a combination of CKD (completely knocked down) kits and their own factory-pressed panels and parts, and there are some interesting differences that make these Aussie-produced buses a little bit quirky. While bus-only clubs are still in their infancy down under, the VW scene itself is very strong, and the Kombi is still renowned for its endurance and versatility in rugged Outback areas.

Ian and Kaye Nankervis are good examples of typical Aussie camper owners who prefer to use their Kombi for adventures rather than the show scene. They are diehard VW fanatics who over the past forty years have had over 250 different VWs! Currently they own around fifty-eight VWs on their twenty-two acre property, but their Split Camper is their pride and joy. Originally imported as a hearse in 1967 (and finished in black) it was a derelict wreck before Ian found it in 2001 and rescued it from the graveyard.

He took just twelve weeks to complete all the work, which included replacing the running gear and brakes with later model items and fitting the interior with a full-width double bed and slide out kitchen. The camper is affectionately known as Desert Splitty and it certainly lives up to its name. In the first eighteen months of owning it they covered 14,000 kms, including a 4,500 kms trip from central Victoria to the Great Sandy Desert in Western Australia, where they lived for nine months before moving 2,500 kms to the Yirrkala Aboriginal Community on the Grove Peninsula. They love getting away into the Outback, especially the desert regions, and every weekend in the dry season (May to November) they are out in the camper, on a deserted beach, camping in a dry river bed, negotiating sand dunes and just enjoying being out in the wilderness. Ian says, 'I just love the look on people's faces when you meet them in a 40-year-old Kombi doing the same thing they are doing in their $60,000 4x4 outfit!'

FIVE BLOKES AND A BUS

In 1993 Matt Keene travelled to Australia, lured by the sun, the surf and stories of rust-free Kombis. Three months later he had acquired a 1966 Aussie-spec Crew Cab pickup truck and had rebuilt its engine, upping the cc to 1600 in the process (Matt has a thing about slow engines). The bus came with a standard Aussie extra – heavy-duty 'roo bars' to protect the front from stray kangaroos. Although designed for commercial use, the double-cab pickup, with its tarpaulin cover, makes a perfect camping vehicle, as bulky gear can be easily slung into the back, and the addition of extra seats behind the driver means five can travel in comfort. While it may not be thought of as a campervan, it can easily be used as one, and some owners have even been known to sleep on the load area – bringing a new meaning to the term 'pick-up bed'.

For the next few months Matt used the Crew Cab as his daily driver, doing temporary work in between checking out all the Sydney surf breaks. During this time he got very friendly with a group of guys staying in the same hostel, all laid back and into surfing. They decided it would be fun to travel across Australia from Sydney to Perth in the bus – 4,500 miles as the crow flies. But that was the direct route. Instead, these guys opted to take the 10,000-mile route right round the coast. The trip took two months in total and there was no plan other than to follow the coast, stopping wherever and whenever they wanted to check out the surf or just soak up the surroundings.

Desert road in South Australia.

They wild-camped out in the bush every single evening, erecting tents and building a campfire. They carried an extra thirteen gallons of fuel in the back of the truck in three jerry cans and also about the same amount of water, as both were difficult to come by in a lot of the remote places they visited. Luckily, the Crew Cab had its original tilt and bows, which proved very useful for carrying all the camping and surfing gear.

The state border between New South Wales and Victoria.

Naturally, being keen surfers, they checked out all of the famous surf breaks en route, such as Bell's Beach, and even spent a week camping at the infamous Cactus point surf spot at Point Sinclair, South Australia. This is possibly one of the most remote surf breaks in the world, as the nearest town is over 200 miles away. Also, being home to a colony of blue whale sharks makes it one of the scariest places in the world to surf.

Some of the highlights of the trip included driving along the Great Ocean Road and across the Nullarbor Plain. Despite peak temperatures on the Nullarbor reaching 118°F, the VW still coped well. Matt changed the oil and serviced the bus three times on the 10,000-mile trip, and they had no breakdowns whatsoever, until they hit the outskirts of Perth at the end of the journey and lost fourth gear for ever. The Crew Cab had served them so well that Matt decided to ship it back to England and, after doing more restoration work, reluctantly passed it on to a new home. Matt says, 'I still see the bus from time to time and it brings a little tear to my eye… but it also brings back many happy memories of when time didn't matter.'

Hanging out in Cremorne Point, Sydney.

Camping in the bush near Bell's Beach, Victoria.

The Concrete Crappa —
somewhere in South Australia!

Near Cactus Point surf spot, Point Sinclair.

The start of the
journey, Sydney.

A KOMBI CLICHÉ

For Ian and Amanda Lloyd, the idea of driving around Australia in a Kombi seemed a bit of a cliché. Apart from not wanting to live up to that cliché, the prospect of driving an air-cooled vehicle in a hot climate seemed crazy to them. What they wanted was something that went, wouldn't cost the earth and would be easy enough to sell at the end of their travels. They had heard all too many horror stories of people not being able to sell their travelling vehicles and almost giving them away just to catch the flight home.

When Ian and Amanda finally arrived in Cairns, in the far north of Queensland, they set about tracking down something suitable to travel round in. After checking out many characterless Mitsubishi L300s and Toyota Hiaces, they began to despair. Then suddenly they saw an ad that read, '1975 Kombi, fresh interior, pop-top, tasty mag wheels' – it seemed there was no escape from the cliché after all! The bus had no interior but seemed very solid. It had a good paint job and the engine sounded sweet. Importantly, it also gave off the right vibe and good feelings, so the next day they parted with around £850 and were ready to begin their adventures. Within a week they had managed to get a basic interior (and bed) sorted out, and finally headed off to explore Australia at their own pace. Ian says:

Clockwise, from top left:

A padamelon pops by in Tasmania.
Ethel in front of Sydney Harbour Bridge.
Snowed in at Cosy Cabins campsite, Tasmania.
A kookaburra keeps Ethel company on a Sydney campsite.
The Pinnacles Desert, Western Australia.
Ethel and Manda by a road sign warning of animals ahead.

I loved our little van, despite its imperfections. The set-up was hardly perfect – we did not have a rock-and-roll bed, and so because the bed was a fixed area it meant that when one of us slept (and by one of us I mean my partner, Manda), the other one had a small area to sit in. The cooler doubled up as a seat for those drinking cold bottles of VB while the other half gently snoozed at nights, and the driver and passenger seats up front became the general dumping ground for anything we didn't need overnight. Although the van wasn't as neatly organised as 'proper' camper conversions, we soon had the routine of setting up for the night and leaving the next day down to a fine art; we didn't trip up over each other, and we never left a campsite so late that we incurred late charges!

From Cairns they headed down the east coast of Australia, then up into the Tablelands around the waterfalls circuit, over to Magnetic Island, through Brisbane and on to Sydney. By now the Kombi had been christened Ethel; well, the Kombi was an old lady and as such needed an old lady name. Ian has fond memories of their travels:

Some of the most magical times in our trip round Australia were linked to our campervan. For example, making our way to Cradle Mountain in Tasmania, as the snow started to fall, quickly turned into something of a blizzard. By the time we arrived at a campsite our toes were freezing and we couldn't wait to get plugged into the mains to get the electric fan heater going. It was all quite spectacular, though, and I'll always remember the curious padamelon [a type of wallaby] sticking his little head

in the van and nibbling the raisins that we left on the side for him. I dare say that if we had bought a newer vehicle to travel around in, we would have spent less on repairs (electrical problems early on in the trip caused us some headaches) but I'm sure that it would not have been quite as much fun.

Ethel was left in Sydney Airport car park while Ian and Amanda toured New Zealand (in a 'proper' motorhome equipped with everything). On their return, reunited with Ethel, they took in Canberra, Melbourne and Tasmania in her before visiting Adelaide and heading off to cross the Nullarbor Plain. This region's name comes from the (pigeon) Latin Nullus Arbor, meaning 'no trees', and is a featureless area that was once the seabed. It also includes the longest straight stretch of road in Australia – 90 miles without a single deviation. Needless to say, Ethel coped superbly.

After eight months' travelling, it was time reluctantly to sell Ethel and return home. She had seen them safely through everything from blizzards to searing heat of over 104°F. But after a lack of any real interest, except from someone in the UK wishing to import her, they decided to keep her and ship her back to England, where she is now faithfully carrying Ian and Amanda to VW shows and on (shorter) holidays. Far from being a cliché, their little VW campervan has won a special place in their hearts, and living with her is now a way of life.

10 WORK, REST AND PLAY

MARTIN CLUNES

It was Michael Parkinson who, on one of his late night chat shows, revealed Martin Clunes' secret passion for VW Campers. Despite being something of a celebrity figure Martin is in fact quite a private man, who has been into the VW bus (though definitely not the VW bus scene) for many years, and who is as passionate about his buses as he is about his TV and film work.

Clunes' first VW bus was a fairly tatty orange camper which he used to run round in during 1992–1993. He did not use it as much as he would have liked, and when asked if he would loan it out for a music TV series in return for a free revamp, he thought why not? When it came back with a shiny new custom paint job Martin decided that, as the bus was now presentable and actually worth something, he would donate it to a charity auction raising money for the Born Free Foundation.

In 1998 he came across a 77 pale blue and white Microbus. Closer inspection revealed that the bus had originally been a double door panel van, which had had side windows cut in. It seemed sound and would fill the gap in his life after parting with his previous bus; he also liked the unusual double sliding door arrangement and the middle seat with flip up ends both sides. It seems to have been used as some kind of minibus for ferrying children round in, judging by the Bugs Bunny sticker warning passengers to exit only from the left side. After a brush with some local white deer, who decided to move the oncoming box on wheels out of their way (and bringing a whole new meaning to the term stag party) Martin decided that the time had come to sort out the bus properly.

The bus was sent to the local restorers, who set to cutting out rust, sorting the deer damage and repainting it. Martin opted to paint the bus in dark navy blue topped with creamy white from the Jaguar colour range. It was only then he realised that the

windows cut into the panel van doors just didn't look right. There was only one option – to fit proper Microbus doors, which were sourced from as far afield as Brazil and Australia. To help combat the never-ending battle with rust, Martin has installed a de-humidifier in his garage, which he hopes will help keep rust at bay (or in this case, not at Bay!).

Martin's other passion is woodwork (not the DIY shelving variety), and for the past few years he has been planning and designing a camping interior for the bus. A rock-and-roll (pull out) bed has finally been fitted and he plans to use an original three-quarter width bulkhead seat unit as a template to make new furniture in cherry wood. Not content with one bus, however, Martin has another pride and joy that is very special and unique: a 1969, all original, double sliding door, walkthrough Deluxe Microbus with just 4,000 miles on the clock. A friend sent Martin and his wife Philippa a catalogue for a forthcoming auction of a private collection at Beaulieu. In it was a picture and details of a Deluxe Microbus, with a range of optional goodies to make any bus buffer go weak at the knees! The price guide was set at between £3,000 and £5,000, so obviously had not been determined by a VW expert. They decided to check it out and the whole family, including the dog, went to the auction. Despite stiff competition from serious collectors, the hammer went down at £10,500 and the bus was theirs. Martin found the auction really exciting and, though he got carried away, he stayed under his ceiling – and even at that price it has to be the steal of the century.

It had originally been part of the collection of Edwin C Jameson Jr., an American Classic Car enthusiast. In August 1969, Jameson contacted a London VW dealership to order a new model Bay window VW bus for his collection. It had to be US spec and the dealership also suggested a range of optional extras to include. Originally Volkswagen informed Jameson

that the non-standard colour black he wanted the bus finished in was not available, but somehow they were persuaded to go along with his request.

The bus was delivered in October 1969 with a US-only spec package including an mph speedo, laminated windscreen, padded dashboard, sealed beam headlights, all red tail lights, reversing lights and anti-dazzle rear view mirror. To this were added twin sliding doors and a retractable side step. As well as being a walkthrough model, additional factory fitted options included an Eberspächer petrol heater, electric fans, heated rear window, whitewall tyres and heavy-duty shocks. When you add all this to a factory sliding metal sunroof, Deluxe chrome trim and upholstery and stunning black paint, you begin to see just how unique and special this bus is. Not only did it have just 3,843 miles on the clock, it also still had the original VW warranty sticker on the cab window, the sticker for the sliding door operation, and even stickers in the engine bay.

What happened to it over the years is unknown, although apparently it was stored in an underground car park to reserve the space for Edwin Jameson's Bentley. This would explain the immaculate condition of the rubbers and seals. However, the whitewall tyres had perished somewhat, due to just sitting around with all that weight on them, and Martin had to replace these, although he decided not to refit new whitewalls as he felt they were a bit garish against the black paintwork.

Martin may not be a bus buffer, but he instinctively knew that this bus was special. He just had to have it. Everything is in mint condition, including the upholstery which came with the factory plastic seat covers still fitted. Little features like the angled side jailbars (on one side only owing to the spare wheel), the low mounted side flashers, the chrome heater outlet surround and the plastic spare wheel cover

Clockwise from centre:
Martin owns two unusual buses, both feature twin sliding doors.
Martin's first camper was given a wild paint job.
Side by side in Thomas Hardy country.
This unique Microbus was stored for 34 years and has only clocked up 4,000 miles.
A village pub makes the perfect stop.

add to its attractions. It certainly deserves the title Deluxe! Driving it is an experience in itself – it's like stepping back in time and driving a brand new bus straight from the showroom. The steering is tight and smooth, the gear change faultless, the ride and handling superb and the brakes actually work, meaning you don't have to drive anticipating stopping ahead of doing it! I have been privileged to drive lots of special buses, from 1951 Barndoor Microbuses to Ladder Trucks and Fire Trucks, but this has to be the most exciting. And scary – especially driving along single-track country lanes flanked by 10-foot high hedges. Martin tactfully refrained from commenting on my driving while quietly removing hedge debris from the air vents. Meanwhile, he loves driving round in the bus, as does daughter Emily who adores sitting up front (in the child's seat) and playing their favourite game: 'What colour is the next Kombi we'll see?'

JAMIE OLIVER

While Martin Clunes' campers enjoy a quiet life pottering round Dorset, Jamie Oliver's Samba is now almost as famous as its owner. Built in 1959, the Samba has a chequered history. It was discovered in 1991, rotting in a scrapyard, by enthusiast Matt Keene, who then set about a four-year restoration on the bus. This involved completely sandblasting the shell and chassis on a rolling jig and replacing all the metalwork. As some repair panels were not available at that time, Matt had to fabricate his own from scratch. A hideous wooden pop top was removed, but luckily the sunroof and slide mechanism just needed refurbishing. A complete interior was sourced from a 1962 Devon camper, and a 1641cc engine featuring a home-made turbo boost set-up, similar to that used on the Renault 5 GTi turbo models was fitted for extra grunt. Matt also fitted front-opening safari windows, pop-out windows all round and an opening rear safari window for the ultimate in cool. The purple and white paint was Matt's work as well.

This special Samba camper was featured in magazines and won awards, but by 1999 Matt was yearning for another project, so the camper passed on to a London music-video producer. During this time it was stolen by a crazy woman, who simply locked it in her garage and polished it every day! The owner was so pleased to get the bus back looking better than when it was stolen that he decided not to press charges.

Campervan owners are used to being asked to sell their bus – people will even approach them at a petrol station or call out at traffic lights asking if it is for sale. So when a young bloke on a scooter knocked on the Samba's window when it was stopped at traffic lights and asked the owner if he wanted to sell it, the driver was not surprised. His response was, 'Only if the price is right'. The young man turned out to be Jamie Oliver, who has a love of classic icons and whose past cars have included a Maserati 4.2 and a Porsche Cayenne.

Being accustomed to fast motors meant that Jamie wanted something even more powerful in the camper. Over the next two years he went through two engines before settling for a custom-built 2.4-litre twin-carb T4 motor with enough power to give the Buses With Attitude boys (see page 17) a scare on the drag strip. Since then, the Samba has featured, with Jamie, in the Sainsbury's TV adverts. (Who can ever forget the one where something is dropped out of a window and smashes through a fake glass roof?) It has also been shown burning round a race track while Jamie frantically tries to prepare a meal in the back. In fact, Jamie's camper has been seen in most of his TV programmes, even ferrying some dinner ladies around in the 'Jamie's School Dinners' series.

It was, however, his 2005 TV series 'Jamie's Italy' that brought the little purple and white camper into everyone's front room. Although many enjoyed watching the cooking or Jamie's enthusiastic full-on style, diehard camper enthusiasts watched just to see the Samba in stunning scenery. With a matching mobile kitchen trailer, built from two Bay Window buses, Jamie toured rural Italy, searching out local culinary delights, which were then demonstrated to the camera. He says of the adventure, 'I've always loved Italy and I wanted to get away from it all, just driving round and cooking.' Among many magic moments, the village where all the children were fed delicious and very healthy school meals based on locally grown organic produce stands out.

Unfortunately, Jamie's camper did not do much for the image of the VW camper, as it decided to behave badly and suffered several breakdowns during the journey, which were all shown on TV along with Jamie's frustration. Things did not start well when, early in the journey, Jamie mistakenly filled the additional crank breather (used to help keep the powerful engine cool) to the brim with oil. At one point Luke Theocari of Terry's Beetle Services, (pictured left with Jamie) who regularly maintains Jamie's camper and keeps it running sweet, even had to fly out to Italy with a replacement gearbox as hand luggage, which he then fitted so that the series could continue. Despite loving his camper, on his return Jamie described his badly behaved camper as 'a pain in the arse' and put it up for sale. Maybe his next series should be about 'handy snacks to sustain you while waiting for the breakdown truck'.

AND WHEN YOU'RE NOT CAMPING IN YOUR BUS...

Ferry your exotic pets in style.

Carry the family canoes.

Originally conceived as a low-cost delivery van, the VW Transporter range quickly extended, and by 1952, included the Microbus and Deluxe Microbus (Samba), the Kombi, the Ambulance and the Pickup truck. Customers quickly began to appreciate the versatility and the reliability of the VW Transporter and in Germany it was even nicknamed the *laste esel* (the colloquialism translates literally as rest donkey). The Kombi version pioneered what is now known as the Multi-Purpose Vehicle (MPV); its easily removable seating and spartan interior made an affordable vehicle to use for business in the week and for the family at weekends.

As seen in Chapter 4, advertisements played on this multi-purpose usage and some camping conversions used the fact that their kit was quickly installable and removable as a key selling point. Other camping conversions were (and still are) marketed specifically as day or weekend vans, with flexible seating arrangements and simple kitchen facilities. The beauty of owning a VW camper is not only in the lifestyle it offers – it also has 1001 practical uses. Ferrying kids on the school run, taking rubbish to the dump, stylish transport to the school prom, carrying engines and parts are just some of the uses owners have found for their buses. Here are a few more...

Answer the age-old riddle 'How many elephants can you fit in a camper?'

Transport the dogs to sheepdog shows and trials.

Set up a stall at a car boot sale.

Collect free firewood for the woodburner.

Collect the local primary school's charity collection of 'Christmas Presents for Africa'.

Take the quad bike and the dog for a spin.

Head off on a garden conservation project.

Save money and time on the hire and erection of scaffolding.

Take granny out for the day.

11 FIRE AND ICE – EXTREME ADVENTURES

Despite Jamie Oliver's experiences in Italy (see page 139), the air-cooled engine that powers the VW camper is legendary for not breaking down (and being easy to fix if it does). This, coupled with the vehicle's high ground clearance, makes the VW ideal for travelling in extreme conditions, whatever the outside temperature or terrain. As can be seen in the travel stories in this book, VW campers navigate places that 4WD vehicles shudder at, and owners have complete faith in their trusty little camper's ability to cope with whatever is thrown at it – sometimes literally. From ice, snow and extreme cold to searing heat and soft sand, the VW camper will never let you down. And if it does, you can always put the kettle on and wait...

SHASTA SNOW TRIP: NOT FOR SISSIES

This trip is not for sissies! Driver teams with endurance, good judgment, mechanical ability and sound machinery will be rewarded with an adventure unlike any ever experienced before. Ever been to a community where people outnumber the teeth and banjos outnumber the hound dogs? We'll pass through several! We're going so far out into the Mendocino, Trinity, Six Rivers and Shasta National Forests that the people still carry side arms. Can your excellent bus make the trip? Do you have the mechanical savvy if you break down 100 miles deep in the Mendocino Forest? If you think you can hack it, then sign up for the Shasta experience now!

Only the hard-core bus driver responds to an advert like that. Leaving comfortable American life behind and heading to northern California to the Shasta National Park in January is now an annual trek for Richard Kimborough, the Rustybus and assorted diehard bus freaks. Mount Shasta is an extinct volcano that stands 14,162 feet high and is 60 miles from the California–Oregon border. Not for the faint-hearted, or even the sane, the Shasta trip captures the American spirit of the past, with man pitting himself against the elements and experiencing extreme danger before emerging triumphantly (if lucky!). The transport of the past is, however, put aside for the modern traveller, and Volkswagen buses and campers are the trusty workhorses for this modern adventure. The trek is a three-day, 1,000-mile endurance trip of dirt, snow and freezing temperatures and can involve up to twenty-four hours' travelling in the first day. Why do it? Well, here's how Richard sees it:

An endurance trip to test the soul and body of both driver and bus. Fun, camaraderie, a sense of accomplishing something real, a trip back to the days of our forefathers, a feat requiring sheer will power to overcome the weather, and the feeling of becoming closer to the world around you.

The trip is full on as soon as it starts, and within minutes, shrouded in darkness, the convoy is weaving uphill on a corkscrew road with a canopy of redwood trees throwing unnerving shadows to confuse the adrenalin-shot drivers. The scenery and weather add to the confusion by changing constantly, with colder than cold turning to sun and heat in an instant. Richard travelled shotgun on his first year with trip organiser Brian Piercy, a caffeinated, high-energy madman and ex-marine who drives his bus like a four-wheeled dirt bike. To get a better photo of the snaking convoy of buses behind them, Richard opened his cargo door and used his Sundial camper's fridge as a step to access the roof of the moving bus. From this vantage point he found himself clinging to the roof as the bus travelled at 35mph down a muddy dirt road in the snow. The snow coated his glasses and the cold seared his bones before Brian stopped to let him back into the passenger seat.

The road unfolds to reveal breathtaking mountain views, with the snowy peaks shrouded in purple clouds looking surreal and reminiscent of scenery from the *Lord of the Rings* movie. At night, as everyone huddles round campfires for warmth and safety, the distant howling of wolves sounds like demented Nazgul and brings a shudder to the bones. Comfortable Middle America seems a lifetime away.

Five years on and Richard is still enthralled by the Mount Shasta experience, but now he drives his own bus, nicknamed the Rustybus. A term used a lot on the Shasta trips is 'opposite lock' – the act of turning your wheels appropriately when sliding on ice. This proves to be excellent fun but requires strong nerves (and brown trousers) as the bus roller-coasters around before pulling out of it in a controlled slide. These mad bus freaks deliberately set out to slide and skid and fishtail as soon as an icy road is encountered. It has been likened to Mr Toad's Wild Ride, as one minute you are sliding gracefully

towards a cliff or sheer drop, then the next minute the wheels grip momentarily and the bus lurches violently back on course.

Richard vividly remembers experiencing this roller-coaster ride for real on the last night of one trip. The area called 4x4 was a 'play area' for trying out sliding stunts and was full of deep puddles that submerged the buses over their lights, plunging the drivers into pitch darkness to continue their stunts. The road was raised and had many paths either side of the 4x4 area. Richard pulled up to the edge of an abyss beside the 4x4 area and his lights were rendered useless as the ground dropped away beneath him. He could not go back as the mud beneath him gave him no traction to reverse. So he continued down the incline feeling as if his bus was standing on its nose. He took it as slow as gravity would allow and managed to reach the bottom unscathed and feeling invincible. With this success still in mind, he drove to another steep incline and steered Rustybus over the top. Soon he realised that the incline was far steeper than the bus was designed to cope with, and Rustybus turned sky rocket, went over the edge and came crashing down nose first, only to bounce back up another five feet in the air and then down again, slamming into the road. Fearing the worst, Richard pulled out of the dive only to find that, apart from damage to the battery tray, Rustybus had come out unscathed. He remarks, 'The blast was indescribable – but not to be repeated!'

Then, of course, there is the Shasta version of the old pioneer-trail river crossings…only now, instead of a covered wagon pulled by oxen, it's a Volkswagen with a 30-horsepower engine. The high ground clearance gives a slight advantage, but the hidden boulders and changes in depth present the same challenges as the early pioneers faced. This time round, though, it's purely for fun. Mad or what?

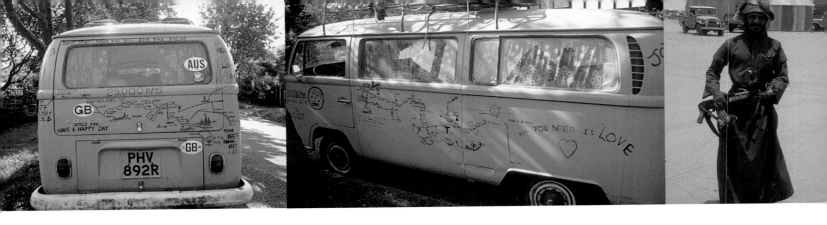

DESERT CROSSING

In 1978 Kevin Jones and John McMahon travelled nearly nineteen thousand miles through Syria, Lebanon, Jordan, Saudi Arabia, Yemen, Qatar and the Arab Emirates. They bought a beaten-up VW Kombi from outside Australia House in London (the place where Antipodean travellers still regularly buy and sell VW vans for overland adventures). The 1970 Kombi had a DIY interior made from plywood and chipboard: primitive but functional. Their objective was to photograph Islamic culture and places of interest for a photolibrary in London. Twenty years later Kevin captured their exploits and journey in a book entitled *Inshallah: Odyssey to the Middle East*. Kevin says of his book:

To write about these adventures and relive them, they are once again becoming fundamentally so much a part of my soul. As the journey through the lands of the Middle East unfolds, I can once again live those moments and am reminded that life can have many paths but that either by accident or design it becomes an adventure. Also one needs a life guide, a truth to believe in, and I found this through the people who helped us in all the countries I visited throughout the Middle East. Our dictum on the road was to always go forward never

back, but this was sorely tested at times. As a general rule we discovered that no matter what the difficulties were we could find solutions ourselves.

The book's title, *Inshallah*, is Arabic for 'It is the will of Allah'. As Kevin says, 'There were certainly quite a few moments in our travels when we could have come to grief but for good luck and an unseen hand helping us on our way.' Many of the 'roads' they travelled on were little more than tracks, or tyre marks in the sand. Yet the VW campervan coped equally well with soft sand or rock-strewn wadis (ravines that are dry except in the rainy season), the high ground clearance and weight at the rear giving it almost 4x4 capability. The following extract from the book gives a flavour of some of the difficulties they encountered when crossing such terrain, in this case negotiating the desert and sand dunes between Yemen and Saudi Arabia:

We followed a set of tracks into the desert that we hoped would take us in the approximate direction of the Saudi border. Many of the lighter vehicles set their own paths across the desert and mistakenly we had followed one of these instead of the main route the lorries took. The consequence of this was

that we hit very soft sand almost immediately and spent a good deal of time digging out. Time to return to Al Bogeh and have a rethink. One particularly bad spot we hit was a sand dyke. This was a long barrier that barred our intended path, far too long to go round and so we made several attempts to get over this and onto the harder sand on the other side.

The dyke itself was about thirty foot high and on several occasions we got to within five to seven metres of the summit before bogging in, having to retrace our steps and try again. We also put markers down to follow, taking advantage of any harder, more compact sand. I just managed to crest the top of the dyke with the VW bottoming out on the sand ridge when, with the engine straining and the clutch spinning to maintain revs, I eventually pulled over the top and to my horror ran full tilt down the unexpectedly steep bank on the other side!

Resisting the temptation to brake my forward speed I just let the Kombi roll down with the help of gravity. Fortunately the drag effect of the sand slowed the vehicle down sufficiently to make a reasonably controlled descent. At the bottom I hit a

gravel bed, hard enough to stop and for John to walk before having a break and thinking about our next move. We were now thoroughly exhausted and becoming paranoid about soft sand which seemed to surround us in every direction. Close by we found some deep ruts left by passing lorries, which we decided was the main route through and which we intended to follow the next day. While I stayed with the van, John walked out to recce the track so we could plan accordingly and aim for an early start. After half a day spent attempting to cross the desert, we had come little further than a few kilometres over the fifty-kilometre route from Al Bogeh to the border.

We waited till well past 8am for a guide, by which time the sun had already gained warmth. The sand had lost its compactness, which results from the cold night chill forming a light dew, and was now little more than 'hourglass' consistency , flowing with the ease of water. We set off down the track, hitting two rather bad sand dykes on the way. With foot to the floor we managed to burst over the tops of them to continue in the wake of the deep ruts left by the passing lorries. Stopping only briefly for a short rest on some more solid ground, we continued along the track until we came to a fork at the foot of a large dune. Taking the left one, as this seemed to follow the directions towards Saudi, we turned a corner to find an enormous dune in front of us. It was a staggering forty foot with a slope of about twenty-five degrees to the top.

We managed to get about halfway up before we bedded in and so we dug out and backed the vehicle down to the bottom. Here we were able to turn the VW round on a gravel shelf and retrace our steps a few hundred yards before turning round and having another attempt. We took several tries, each time churning up even more sand and becoming stuck, still only about halfway up the dune. On one occasion, as we took the sharp left bend by the fork, I was probably going no more than 30kph but with all the weight on board the VW, we still went up onto two wheels until the back end slewed round. Applying opposite lock we lost a lot of momentum and managed to get only a few feet up the dune that particular time.

By now our nerves were becoming frayed and also the sand had now become so churned up on the dune that we were gradually getting further and further from the top on each attempt. We decided to give it one more go and wherever we stuck we would dig our way out to the top. We got halfway up the slope before the back wheels started to dig in. I immediately stopped and we jumped out, pulling all the available matting from inside the vehicle with us, rubber floor mats, carpets, towels anything that would give support and traction to the wheels. Extricating ourselves was a tedious process of digging sand from under the vehicle, placing the mats to the front wheels and driving slowly. We had to slip the clutch to give a gradual take-up of power and were only able to climb a further five to ten feet at a time.

This all took place under the blazing heat of the desert sun, very much like the scene in the classic movie *Ice Cold in Alex*. It was a laborious process

and extreme care had to be taken so as to prevent the rear wheels getting bogged down. If this were to occur we would probably have had to run back to the bottom of the dune and start all over again. Time and again we would carefully jack up the rear wheels, fill in the ruts underneath, lay mats on top and, after lowering the wheels back down, coax the VW a little further. Just as we were calculating how much longer we would be on this stretch, a four-wheel-drive Toyota Land Cruiser came by and offered us a tow, but said that he had no tow rope! He was quite adamant that very soon we needed to clear the route as lorries would pass this way and that he would help us for 100 SR (about £14 sterling)... a bargain! Using the six metres of chain that held all our jerry cans to the roof rack, with a struggle and both engines revving hard, the Toyota managed to pull us to the top and we were finally able to stand on relatively firm sand to unhitch the chain. We paid the driver, who left us to our own devices as we sat down to have a breather, a cup of chai and of course a cigarette, to calm the already strained nerves. The route we rejoined was very much as we remembered, with deeply rutted sand tracks but steerable if taken carefully. No matter, we were on our way, thankful to be back on level ground and what appeared to be the correct track.

(The book *Inshallah*, which recounts the full story of the overland adventures, can only be obtained direct from Kevin Jones, 30 Pine Gardens, Upton on Chester, Chester CH2 1DB, England or www.tele-mation.co.uk)

DESERT CROSSING

149

Forget thoughts of barefoot hippies with beads – today's camper lovers go for the full-on classic style of wedding, but now the Rolls-Royce, or horse and carriage, has been replaced with a classic camper. If you live with a bus and are getting married, there really is only one way to go: use your camper as the wedding transport for the bride and bridesmaids. What better way to celebrate the central role of buses in your future relationship – which will in turn, no doubt, create the next generation of bus babies.

AND A FUNERAL

But it's not only bus lovers and fanatics who get married with a bus. A growing number of people just love the classic look and yearn for nostalgia and the idea of something a little different for their special day. The resurgence of interest in the VW camper today is such that there are now several companies which will organise and provide wedding/bride transport, from an immaculately dressed sunroof Samba to a stretched white Limo-Beetle!

NOT JUST A HIGHLAND FLING

Rikki James is one of those people who live, eat, sleep and dream buses. Back in 1979, at the rebellious age of nineteen, he borrowed his father's camper and headed off to the beaches at Biarritz. Despite pester power he was never able to persuade his dad to pass it on to him. It would be ten years before he would finally own his own Split camper – a purple and white Samba (Deluxe Model with sunroof, roof skylights and windows all round) which he decked out with Warhol-style banana-print material and christened the Banana Bus. Rikki and his wife-to-be Viv travelled all over in this bus,

including an epic six-month European tour. By the 1990s they were both heavily involved in the bus scene, and Rikki took on the role of Special Display coordinator for the Splitscreen Van Club, organising line-ups and displays of Split campers at shows and events. One of the most famous was an impressive line-up of one model of bus from every year from 1950 to 1979.

Since the Banana Bus, Rikki has owned a 1965 Samba, the Herbie Bus (complete with 53 decal as in the original Disney Herbie Beetle) and a 1958 Samba.

He currently runs the Musclebus, a 1954 RHD Samba (very rare) complete with period Swedish camping interior and a 2.6 litre Type 4 Porsche 914 motor for extra grunt. This bus is seriously fast and has clocked sixteen seconds on the quarter-mile drag strip. Rikki is also a founder member of BWA (Buses With Attitude) – to join, you have to run the quarter-mile in a pre-1967 bus in under eighteen seconds.

As Viv hails from Aberdeen, that was the only possible location for their marriage in July 1998. Of course, the wedding vehicles had to be Sambas – three, in fact. No Scots wedding is complete without the groom in a kilt. Luckily the MacDonald Tartan is one of the two allowed to be worn by Sassenachs (the English) and other foreigners, and very fetching it looks too. And the honeymoon? What else but a tour of the Scottish Highlands in the Herbie Bus, accompanied by three other vintage campers. And if you think one looks suspiciously like Jamie Oliver's camper, you are right – only here it was with its previous owner, who had driven for thirteen hours straight, arriving just in time to be fitted with a kilt before commencing bridesmaid-transport duties.

Rikki can't imagine life without his camper. He says, 'I love the versatility, the scene, the vibe, the people, hooking up with buddies every weekend. But the best part is, if you drive a Split bus it just makes people smile!'

Previous pages, from left to right:

For your business, for your wedding, get a VW bus!
Herbie rides again – reborn as a camper.
Buses on parade.
The bus community pay tribute to a much-loved enthusiast.

VOLKS WEDDING

In 2000 Andrew Fowler got back into the veedub scene after a ten-year break and bought a 1981 Type 25 Danbury camper. The camper's tired old curtains needed some attention so Andrew asked his gran to run up some new ones. Obligingly, she did just that and this kick-started a new business, VW Curtains. At that time Andrew was an IT consultant and so it was easy for him to produce a website, following which his business was born. Meanwhile, Andrew had met Kay and together they had a baby daughter called Lauren. As the business went from strength to strength so did their relationship, and soon they set the date for their wedding in May 2005. Kay shared Andrew's love for all VWs, and it was agreed that the wedding vehicles must be VW campers.

On the wedding day Kay arrived in a 1961 New Zealand Devon camper which was owned and restored by Mark Soar. Andrew took his restored 1967 panel van, a Swedish import stock 1500. His best man had a 1994 993 Carrera 2, which was also owned by Andrew. After the wedding, the business continued to grow and Kay and Andrew became business partners as well as marriage partners, with Kay handling all the mail order side and the administration. They continue to be part of the VW family, attending shows and meets with the Trade Stand. They like the VW lifestyle because of the friendly scene, and they like to keep, in Andrew's words, 'the cool old vans on the road and not in the scrapyard'.

A WEDDING DOWN UNDER

This wedding is a classic example of the way the bus community all over the world help each other out. Sam and Kelly have both been bus freaks ever since they can remember, and when planning their wedding in Perth, Western Australia, they wanted to make a classic VW bus part of the special day. Sam posted a message on a VW forum asking if anyone could help out and immediately had a reply from 'Simon.in.oz' offering his white T25. Simon then put Sam in contact with Paul, the owner of a mint 1964 Split Microbus. A phone call to Paul later and they had the bride's transport sorted.

They met up with Paul and his wife Sandy in March 2005, a few days before the wedding, and found them friendly and helpful. The bus was absolutely immaculate. Sam decorated the bus in traditional style with some pink ribbon and Paul added the bow as a finishing detail. On the wedding day Paul picked up the bride-to-be, two bridesmaids, one flowergirl and the kilt-wearing ring-bearer, Callum, and treated them all to a ride down Perth's beautiful coastline in the sun. Sam and Kelly say, 'It was a fantastic day, and made all the more special by the kindness of Paul and Sandy and their fabulous Splitty.'

Sam and Kelly Carter have now set up in business as Pop Scene, specialising in pop-art-style paintings of VWs. Sam describes their work:

'Inspired by both a lack of affordable/quality Volkswagen imagery at shows and an interest in experimenting with artistic techniques, we hope that the canvases we've created will show that delicious eye-candy can be utterly original and still not cost the earth'.

Campers are clearly in their future for a very long time to come.

LOVE AFFAIR AMERICAN STYLE

Isaiah Hanback was hooked on buses from the tender age of fifteen, and was well on the way to becoming a fully fledged fanatic by sixteen. He was introduced to Der Busbesitzer Gruppe, and his bus interest and friendships flourished. His girlfriends wouldn't put up with his hobby until he met Tasha, who, although not overly interested in getting dirty

doing restoration work, would watch the process keenly as their 1961 flipseat Westfalia camper was restored to its former glory.

In 2003 their pride and joy won 'Best Bus' at the Buses Nowhere Near the Arch meet. Meanwhile Isaiah and Tasha's relationship had flourished, and

they set their wedding day for 18th September 2004. Isaiah bought an early wedding gift of a 1957 black Oval ragtop Beetle and compiled a guest list that included all his bus buddies (and their vehicles). Billy Knudson was asked to be best man as he was responsible for Isaiah's involvement with Der Busbesitzer Gruppe five years earlier.

The wedding guests were asked to drive a VW to the wedding and they were taken on a pre-wedding cruise around Oshkosh, Wisconsin, ending up at Lake Winnebago. The photo line-up at the lake included three roof-hatch Westfalia campers, a '67 and a '72 Westfalia, a '71 sunroof standard bus, the legendary John Lago's '62 custom bus, plus a few assorted Beetles and buses that also turned up for the reception party.

Tasha and Isaiah left for their honeymoon in a 1978 Porsche 911SC (borrowed from the guy who sold them their early wedding present Beetle). They spent a week in Door County, Wisconsin, starting married life on the road touring. Isaiah now runs a VW workshop and puts his prosperity and marriage down to his first love affair with VWs. As he says, 'If it weren't for buses I wouldn't be working in the field I am now, I wouldn't have all the great friends I have now, I wouldn't have the home I have now and may not even have the wife I have now.'

IN THE MIDST OF LIFE...

In the same way that the bus community comes together to celebrate, it also comes together to pay tribute and mourn. Ben 'Boatyard' Bosworth was one of those people totally into living with their buses. More than anything he loved hunting out rare period parts, trinkets and 'bus junk', which meant that his van changed every time you saw it. The Boatyard Bus was well known (and much photographed) at shows and events, as Ben would go to every show, surf mission or camping trip possible.

His bus was actually one of the first Devon conversions from 1957, built as a demonstration model, and was in a sad way when he acquired it in 2000. Despite suffering from lifelong chronic renal failure, Ben rebuilt the van just about entirely himself with the help of a few friends over a period of three years, working on it at weekends and on as

many evenings as he could spare. Strict medical regimes and dirty buses are a difficult mix, but nothing could stop Ben doing what he loved.

The van debuted at VW Action in 2003, twenty-five years after it had last been on the road. Being such a rare and desirable bus, which so few people knew of, meant that there were a lot of interested faces surrounding it all weekend. Ben was one of the first to pioneer what has become known as the Rat Look, and his seriously lowered, scruffy paint and 1776cc-engine-powered camper set the 'standard' for other Rats to emulate.

Sadly, Ben died from his illness in June 2005, aged just thirty-two. The bus community turned out in force to pay homage, and some friends even borrowed a VW hearse (albeit a customised one)

from contacts in Belgium; it was used in the funeral cortege. Inspired by the friendship, help and self-esteem Ben found in the VW bus scene, Ben's parents and some VW friends have since set up the Ben Bosworth Memorial Fund, specifically for people in the air-cooled VW scene who are suffering from 'need, hardship or distress caused by illness'. At the time of writing the Memorial Fund is being set up, but the kinds of areas funding could be allocated to would range from holiday insurance for someone suffering from a serious health problem to ensure otherwise prohibitively expensive temporary treatment would be available, to funding equipment that cannot be supplied through state health-care provision. A fitting memorial to a brave young man who got immense pleasure from living the VW camper scene to the max and a reminder to all that in the midst of life...

13 OUT OF AFRICA: AN EPIC JOURNEY

Ever since learning at school about Cecil Rhodes' vision of a Great North Road cutting through Africa from Cape Town to Cairo, Christian Figenschou had dreamed about travelling this route. In the early 1990s he got into VW campers and decided that an old Splitty would be the ideal vehicle for this adventure. Life and careers got in the way, but then suddenly in 2001 he found himself redundant and decided now was the time to go for it and pursue his dream.

Over the years he had made all sorts of plans for the modifications he would need to make to a camper, but he soon realised this fantasy bus would cost the earth to equip. What he did have, however, was a recently restored 1975 Fleetline Kombi, a 60s throwback, hybrid, fifteen-window Splitscreen bus, made in Brazil and assembled in South Africa. Part Splitty, part Bay, the bus was totally stock apart from having been painted up in zebra stripes like the old East African safari buses.

Christian, his partner Gisela and their travelling companions Shaun and his girlfriend Gina set off from Johannesburg in July 2002 on the coldest day of the year. They headed down to Cape Agulhas, Africa's southernmost point, which was the formal starting point of the journey. From there the Zebra Bus made for Cape Town, where they unpacked everything and sent some things back home to lighten the load. North of Cape Town they travelled to a semi-desert region called Namaqualand. Timing their arrival perfectly for just after the rains, they found the entire area carpeted with riotous colour from millions of wild flowers now in bloom.

From here the planned journey would take them across Namibia, Botswana, Zambia, Malawi, Tanzania, Kenya, Ethiopia, Sudan and Egypt, and then they would cross into Europe. At this point Gina found the thought of the journey ahead a little daunting and returned home.

In Botswana, they made a four-day safari in *mokoros* (dug-out canoes) into the Okavango Delta, a unique paradise surrounded by the sands of the Kalahari Desert and undoubtedly one of the world's finest unspoilt wildernesses. The Kavango River rises in Angola but, instead of proceeding to the sea, reaches maturity in the Kalahari Desert, where it drains into the desert sands in the world's only inland delta, to create a vast, waterlogged Garden of Eden teeming with wildlife. Then it was over the Zambezi by ferry and into Zambia. Christian kept a diary of their travels and picks up the story from this point:

Next we headed to Zambia's capital, Lusaka, where we spent a few days with friends, before moving east, to the South Luangwa National Park. In Lusaka we were arrested and briefly held by military police after Shaun alighted from the bus in sight of a military barracks while brandishing a camera. We were eventually released after an hour-long interrogation with a warning that Zambians are 'very sensitive about photography'. As we drove across Zambia we discovered that the country's formerly notorious potholed roads are being repaired and rebuilt, and many of the worst stretches have now been refurbished. Driving across Zambia we also encountered a hazard that many people had warned us about: regular police and army roadblocks. These checkpoints are set up less in the interests of national security than with the intent to extort cash and 'gifts' from travellers. We dealt with all requests for 'gifts' by simply saying no, which was always an acceptable answer.

In Tanzania we had our first tangle with the police, when a cop pulled us over while we were crawling through a village and accused us of speeding. He was determined to extract some payment from us as penalty for our 'transgression'. We were determined to give the cop nothing. The situation developed into a tense stand-off, before the cop gave up, saying he would 'forgive us this time'. Luckily this experience was offset by the 'high' of climbing Mount Kilimanjaro, Africa's highest peak, and all three of us made it to the 5,895m summit at Uhuru Peak, which was a very emotional experience. We descended from the literal high point of our journey straight to the emotional lowest point, in the nearby town of Moshi.

On our last night in Tanzania, Shaun and I left our campsite in Moshi in the early evening to walk to a nearby restaurant to get takeaways. It turned out to be further away than it had appeared when driving in the car, but it was less than two kilometres, so we pressed on regardless. Our walk took us through a very dark patch over a bridge across a river, but we met nobody on the way. However, on the walk back with the food, we heard people down the embankment under the bridge. There was nothing obviously threatening about this, but we both felt unsafe and quickened our pace. We could hear someone climbing the embankment and walking on the bridge behind us and we kept walking fast. Then suddenly two men came up quickly behind us. They seemed drug-crazed and afraid, and they jabbered at us in Swahili while one of them grabbed at my arm and the other shone a torch in my face. I pulled away and turned to face them, still walking fast, backwards, and they repeated whatever they had said to us. It was obvious they were not making friendly conversation and their fear was quite palpable. One of them tugged at my arm again and I pulled away once more, this time warning him to keep out of my space. Something was obviously wrong, but it was not clear what.

Right: Christian, Gisela, Shaun and Gina ready to set off on the coldest day of the year.

Previous pages, from left to right:
Zambian roads are notorious for potholes and rocks.
Crossing the Equator in Kenya.
Wild elephants grazing at the roadside, Zambia.
Stuck in sand in the Nubian Desert, Sudan.

Top left: *The road surface was so bad that urgent welding repairs were needed. Mud was used to protect the surrounding areas.*

Top right: *The Trans East African Highway in Kenya – the road from hell.*

Below: *Watch out for marauding camels!*

anywhere. We thanked him and said we would be OK, as we were only about a hundred metres from the camp.

Our entrance to the camp caused a wave of consternation as I staggered in with my head and face and shirt drenched in blood. People gathered all around to help or ogle, until Gisela shooed them away, asking them to give us some space. One of the onlookers demanded of us, 'What were you thinking, walking out here in the night? This is a very dangerous area.' What were we thinking indeed? In the light I saw that Shaun had a deep cut on his chin from the first rock, and I was still pouring blood over everything. We should have gone to a hospital, but we were all too shaken to move. Meanwhile, Gisela dressed Shaun's chin and cleaned my head up. Despite all the blood, my wound was not serious, just a heavily lacerated bruise. Shaun should probably have had a couple of stitches on his chin. Once we had calmed down we realised we had got off lightly. There were no serious injuries and we had not given the robbers anything. I took it as a gentle nudge from the universe to remember where I am. I had been getting too comfortable. Yes, most Africans are friendly and welcoming, but this is still a dangerous continent, where life is cheap.

In Nairobi (known locally as Nairobbery!) we moved in with my cousin Daphne, a well-known wildlife artist. Nairobi was a period of emotional breakdown for us. The stress of travelling so long with three people in a confined space was beginning to tell. And the mugging in Moshi had brought up a lot of fears for Shaun. Eventually, after working through a

Then the mood shifted up a gear, although I can't say what made it apparent. A car was coming towards us, and Shaun stepped into the road to wave it down, but it swerved away and roared past. I was still facing the pair when, in the same moment, one of them threw something at Shaun and the other drew something from a bag, which appeared in the dark to be a weapon of some sort. In that moment it was finally fully apparent that we were under attack and we both simultaneously began running away and yelling for help. I had run about twenty metres when I felt a terrific blow on the back of my head and saw stars. I blacked out momentarily and came to with my legs collapsing under me and my body pitching forward, out of balance. One of the attackers had thrown a fist-sized river stone at me, and had scored a direct hit. Unconsciousness seemed such an inviting place but, with a huge effort of will, I called the strength back to my legs and corrected my balance and managed to keep running, as I felt the warm, treacly flow of blood running down my neck and soaking into my shirt.

Then suddenly there was a looming shape in the darkness... a broken-down truck, and a man was running up, asking us what was wrong. We explained that someone had tried to rob us. The man was horrified and clearly concerned, and offered to take us to hospital and the police, but he was also obviously feeling helpless, as his truck was broken down and he could not take us

164

lot of issues in the group, Shaun elected to return home. Shaun's departure cleared the air and substantially lightened the Zebra Bus, just as we prepared to head into the real wild Africa. Up to Nairobi the roads are good and the going is fairly easy, with English spoken everywhere, and most of the necessaries of modern life obtainable. But north of the equator the good roads come to an end, and English ceases to be the lingua franca.

The first day out of Nairobi we crossed the equator, and camped that night in the grounds of a motel at Chogoria, on the slopes of Mount Kenya. After a leisurely start the next day, we covered the last 150 kilometres to Isiolo, where the asphalt ends, and the road from hell begins...

One can cover the whole distance from Cape Town to Nairobi on paved roads. Some are badly potholed, but there's no reason why one couldn't do the journey in the family hatchback. However, north of Isiolo, there are very few paved roads; from northern Kenya, through all of Ethiopia and Sudan, until Egypt, most of the 'roads' range from rough tracks to rocky trails. And the first stretch is arguably the worst. This two-day route, covering five hundred kilometres from Isiolo, through Marsabit, to Moyale on the Ethiopian border, is ironically named the Trans East African Highway. The 'highway' is hard as concrete, mercilessly corrugated, and paved with a loose scree of razor-sharp broken lava, which is piled up into a middle hump as high as truck axles. This brutal track is infamous as a shredder of tyres and destroyer of vehicles. The route crosses the Dida Galgalu Desert, a region crawling with Shifta bandits, and one is obliged to travel in convoy.

Although our eight-ply Goodyear tyres withstood the assault of broken lava, the rest of the car took some serious wear and tear. The bodywork cracked above the rear hatch and along the gutter, several of the roof-rack legs cracked, the exhaust tailpipe broke off, and we made regular stops to retighten exterior mirrors, bumpers and even wheel bolts that had vibrated loose. We spent an extra day at the halfway point of Marsabit so we could have the damaged bodywork welded up. From Marsabit to Moyale, the Kenyan police would only let us pass the checkpoints with an armed guard on board, so we drove that stretch with a policeman in the car, armed with a G3 automatic rifle.

When we finally crossed into Ethiopia at Moyale, we were overjoyed to find an asphalt road that leads all the way to Addis Ababa. It was very uneven and potholed in sections but, after what we'd been through, it felt like an autobahn. Ethiopia left us speechless with wonder at its magnificent and varied scenery, its ancient culture, and its fascinating, though very wild, people. I was pleasantly surprised, when we reached Addis Ababa, to find the city full of old air-cooled Volkswagens. Most were in a very dilapidated condition, but nonetheless I spotted Splitscreen buses every day on the roads of Addis, as well as many Beetles from the 1960s and even a handful of oval windows.

From Addis we headed northwards again. We soon discovered that the road from Moyale to Addis is one of only two paved roads in the entire country, and that there are no paved roads at all north of the capital. Most major routes are very difficult, and minor routes are no more than donkey tracks. From Addis we made our slow way northwards to Bahir Dar and Lake Tana, site of many island monasteries, one of which is apparently the resting place of the Ark of the Covenant. Ethiopian Christianity dates back more than a millennium, and Ethiopians are very proud that they were Christians when most of Europe was still in the Dark Ages.

From Bahir Dar we continued on to Gondar, with its medieval castle and cathedral, and then into Sudan. But not without drama... The first time we left Gondar, we were about fifty kilometres out of the town when we noticed a terrible clattering noise from the engine. It turned out the cooling fan had cracked around the hub. Despite the infernal racket, the fan was still turning, so we were able to return to Gondar. Then followed a wild goose chase as we sought out a good, used replacement fan. We did find two of them, but the Ethiopian garage owners thought we were desperate and priced them accordingly. Eventually I removed the damaged fan (without pulling the engine) and had it welded up for a token fee. However, while I was removing the carb to make space to get the alternator and fan out, I dropped a small washer down the manifold without noticing. When I started the engine after reassembly it made a loud ringing noise. DOH! There was nothing for it but to pull the engine and do a partial strip down to remove the offending washer, which delayed us another day.

The 400-kilometre stretch from Gondar to Al Gederif in Sudan is the only open route between Ethiopia and Sudan, and is notoriously difficult, becoming largely impassable in wet weather. It is being rebuilt in stretches, but remains a challenging drive. At Al Gederif we intersected the paved road between Port Sudan and Khartoum, and we made good time to the capital, where we stayed for a few days while we organised our Egyptian visas. We spent Christmas in Khartoum, before heading north once more. Our route out of Khartoum followed a new paved road that was not on our maps, and about 350 kilometres north of the capital the road ended summarily in the middle of the Nubian Desert.

From there to Wadi Halfa near the Egyptian border there are no roads at all, just sandy trails through the desert and a stony track alongside the Nile. This 650-kilometre stretch took us five days of driving, ten hours a day, the whole way in second gear! The first hundred kilometres after the paved road ended involved ploughing through deep sand. The Zebra Bus amazed us with its off-road prowess, and we got stuck in the sand only six times. On two of those occasions we had to use our makeshift sand ladders to get ourselves unstuck but, the rest of the time, we were helped by passing trucks or villagers. In the desert of Sudan no one ever passes you by without first establishing that you're OK. In Sudan we found the kindest, most hospitable people in Africa. We were constantly being accosted by strangers who spoke

Crossing Lake Nasser by cargo boat.

no English, but who insisted we come into their homes for meals or refreshments and who gave us gifts without expecting anything in return. By the time we finally reached the dusty, desert frontier town of Wadi Halfa we were exhausted. But we had an enforced rest as we had to wait twelve days for a cargo barge to carry us across Lake Nasser to Aswan in Egypt.

Egypt is serviced by a network of good asphalt roads, and they rejoiced to be able to drive in fourth gear again. From Aswan they drove up the Nile to Luxor, where they visited the Valley of the Kings and the temples of Luxor, Karnak and Hatshepsut, before veering off to the Red Sea, where they went scuba diving on the pristine coral reef at Sharm el Naga. By the time they rolled triumphantly into Cairo, they had been on the road for more than six months, and had driven twenty-two thousand kilometres since leaving Johannesburg. Their first view of the Great Pyramids at Giza was a very emotional moment, as it marked the end of their Cape to Cairo adventure. They had successfully crossed the second largest continent on earth on a wing and a prayer in an ancient vehicle, without a single breakdown or puncture – an epic journey in anyone's book.

From here they had planned to cross Libya and take a ferry to Italy from Tunisia, but after endless wrangles about visas and with their Egyptian visas about to expire, they finally had to cut their losses and head for Europe via the Middle East and Turkey. They were already three months behind schedule and this meant adding ten thousand kilometres and ten more border crossings. But, as Christian says, 'The destination had suddenly become more important to us than the journey.'

In Jordan they had their first major engine problem: low-grade petrol, combined with hot weather and a 250-kilometre ascent from sea level to 1,750 metres caused severe detonation and overheating. Despite their retarding the timing and stopping frequently to let the engine cool, the engine suffered terminal damage, culminating in valve meltdown just outside Aleppo. Ever prepared and resourceful, Christian stripped the engine in a side street and found that the broken valve had fortunately not holed the piston. He fitted a spare cylinder head brought for just such a contingency and had the bus running again the same day. But the impact of the piston hitting the broken valve head had caused a hairline crack in the piston. The next day, in a remote region of the Turkish countryside, the damaged piston disintegrated, all but destroying the engine.

Luckily they got a tow back to Gaziantep, where they found an air-cooled backstreet VW 'garage'. A strip down showed that the bits of broken piston had damaged all the other pistons and cylinders, but fortunately there was no other internal damage to the engine. As there were no new parts available in Gaziantep, the mechanic rebuilt the engine with a set of used pistons and cylinders from his carefully hoarded stash of scrap. But the parts were worn out, and although the repair got the Zebra Bus running again, the engine was very sick. It smoked badly, number four spark plug oiled up regularly, and there was a nasty oil leak.

They limped on and crossed Turkey in two days. They nursed the bus as far as Vienna, where local VW contacts, who had been following their story on the internet, rallied round to offer aid and support. However, by the time they entered Germany the bus was suffering from serious power loss and the oil leak was now leaving a slick large enough to send the local bird population into panic!

The journey came to an abrupt end in Stuttgart. They were pulled over by the Polizei, who took one look at the travel-worn Zebra Bus and its dishevelled occupants and promptly took the bus to the local TUV (German equivalent of an MOT test) station. There the inspectors catalogued a list of faults as long as the journey they had just travelled. The police then imposed heavy on-the-spot fines and, to add insult to injury, impounded the registration papers and number plates, thus ensuring the poor old Zebra Bus could never drive in the EU again. Their parting comment, as they left Christian and Gisela despondent at the roadside was, 'Remove that dangerous junk or it will be towed to a scrapyard – at your expense!' It must have been a heart-rending moment to endure such an ignominious end to the VW that had carried them all the way through Africa and into Europe. Fortunately Michael Steinke, a respected German bus guru and enthusiast, managed to persuade a friend to take the Zebra Bus into his private collection which is where it still resides today.

The journey had taken ten months of hard travelling, totalling thirty-one thousand kilometres across three continents. Christian had fulfilled his dream, and his adventure of a lifetime is something he will doubtless share with his future grandchildren.

The Great Pyramid, Giza.

Christian had to rebuild the engine on the streets of Aleppo, Syria.

Camping in the New White Desert, Egypt.

The end of the road: German police declare the Zebra Bus dangerous and impound it.

14 TRIBAL GATHERINGS

Fifty-six years on, the VW camper is more popular and fashionable than ever. The 'holiday cottage on wheels' has come a long way in that time, and the bus scene today is very different. While the appeal of the weekend away or family holiday is still part of the attraction, it's the spirit of community that has evolved and grown. That's why VW bus owners flash their lights at each other and have a special wave: they share an affinity for something unique.

Although getting away into the countryside for family weekends or hitting the beach with a group of friends is still what owning a camper is all about, for many campervan owners the year also now revolves around travelling to the many different VW shows. Until the 1990s the VW Beetle ruled supreme at the dozen or so VW events in the UK, but times have changed. A glance round any event field these days will show this is the time of the VW bus, in particular the campervan. Starting with the aptly named DubFreeze in February (for which some diehards actually camp), nearly every weekend for the next eight months has a show of some kind. Many events run from Friday through till Sunday (plenty of time for serious partying), but even the 'one-day' shows usually have overnight camping and entertainment laid on.

Some shows are tailored specifically for the VW bus tribe to come together and celebrate their buses – notably Vanfest (which now draws over three thousand campervans each year) and Bus Types in the UK and the OCTO Show in California. However, there are also many VW shows where Beetles, Karmann Ghias, Trekkers, etc, all rub shoulders with the ubiquitous VW camper. These events bring the whole VW Nation together – a vintage Beetle parks next to a New Beetle, Golfs are on display next to pickups and panel vans, and campers and cabriolets snuggle up to each other. And what better way to enjoy the show than living comfortably in your campervan all weekend, as opposed to sleeping in a tent and eating fast food? Who cares about rain or mud when there is a warm bus waiting for you?

Many VW owners belong to a local or national club; as well as the social side, clubs provide many services such as discounts, spares and regalia, lively magazines, and access to endless technical help and advice. When they are not travelling to an event together, they will be convoying off to camp somewhere. At events, clubs park up together and often put on special displays. Owning a vehicle is prized, but sharing it and showing it off are just as important. What's the use of owning a rare Van Gogh if you can't display it in an art gallery for all to admire? It's the same for a good many bus owners, who go to shows to 'show off' their pride and joy, or to simply enjoy and be inspired by what others have done to their vehicles.

Event organisers know their audience (and, unlike other types of show, share their passion), and as well as live music or retro discos they also cater for families, with quiet camping areas and activities such as face painting, hair braiding, clowns, colouring competitions and fun races, and run inter-club competitions such as five-a-side football.

Opposite: VW action – a Dubhenge sculpture.

Going to a show not only gives you the chance to relax and renew friendships, but you can also do your parts-shopping al fresco, exercising as you tramp miles around showgrounds feeling good about your outdoor lifestyle. Every show has a different vibe, with some catering for the loud, young and noisy while others are pitched at the older, more serious buffers, or families where kids and pets are to the fore. From vintage shows (where even a missing correct-year tool-roll can mean losing the Best In Class award) and small informal shows with a laid-back atmosphere, to huge festival-type events with live entertainment all weekend, the show scene is now an essential part of the VW lifestyle.

Younger campervan owners love the drag strips, racing buses with serious engines around tracks. They like late-night bands and parties, sleeping in well past morning coffee. The family groups love shows with quiz nights and theme nights where all take part in dressing up and partying with lots of food, food, food and disco muzak. They emerge well in time for morning coffee and get all the best bargains in the auto-jumbles.

The more classic-orientated owners are catered for at events like Brighton Breeze or Stanford Hall, which provide daytime activities of polishing and showing vehicles and an opportunity to see rare displays in lovely rural and seaside settings. Brighton Breeze has an added bonus – not only do you convoy with seven hundred VW buses from London, but you also get parked up right along the seafront, making a stunning display. Shows such as BVF pride themselves on a family feel, while others like VW Action are full-on weekends with funfair, comedy tents and several music tents – serious partying!

The trade sections at shows nowadays reflect the changes. Where once the oily, rusty auto-jumble reigned supreme, now you will find anything and everything to do with the VW lifestyle, from clothing to jewellery, from teapots to children's beds shaped like a camper... plus, maybe, that part you have been waiting to find for years.

European shows have a different feel again, and offer an alternative setting for British buses, as well as an opportunity to see some of the many rare vehicles

that seem to abound across the channel. With a cold beer or glass of wine, language barriers simply melt away as groups get together in a leisurely manner, which feels like a holiday, to talk technical specs, work on engines, or inspect interiors. The German and Dutch bus enthusiasts in particular are a very hospitable people and offer beers and chat while readily opening up their buses to all.

The American shows tend to be very different, often being one-day events that usually take place in parking lots and are over by mid-afternoon. However, the same vibe and friendship exist – what better way to spend time than in the company of others who share your obsession (or is it addiction?) and admire the diversity that exists in the VW bus world?

Whatever the show, in whatever part of the world, one thing is common to all: an eclectic mix of young and old, from all walks of life, enjoying the friendship, freedom and fun that come from being part of the VW Nation. Obsession or addiction, they are all crazy about their campers – or should that read Campervan Crazy?

INDEX

Former teachers Dave and Cee Eccles have been around VW Campers since 1976, when they bought a Splitscreen camper, gave up their teaching jobs and spent a year living and travelling in it through Persia and Afghanistan to Kashmir and India. Two years later they bought a 1966 Devon camper, which they then owned and kept in original condition for 34 years, travelling all over Europe and the UK with their children, before finally selling it in 2012 to buy a new T5 California camper.

Dave has been editor of *Volkswagen Camper and Commerical* magazine since it was founded in 2001 and is the author of several books about the VW bus, notably *VW Camper: The Inside Story* – a detailed guide to interior conversion and camping models from their introduction in 1951.

Despite no longer owning an iconic Splitscreen campervan, Dave and Cee are still fully immersed in the VW bus scene and help organise the magazine's big VW Bus show at Weston Park – Camperjam; only nowadays they cruise to shows and holidays in comfort! However, the journey is still as important as the destination… in the immortal words of Mr Toad: "Here today, up and off to somewhere else tomorrow! Travel, change, interest, excitement! The whole world before you, and a horizon that's always changing!"

Acknowledgements and credits

We should like to thank all those owners whose campers and interiors are shown here and to credit and thank the following people who supplied us with additional pictures. If we have inadvertently omitted to mention anyone, please let us know for any future edition.

Additional photographs courtesy of:
Julian Hunt, Anna Slydell, Ralph Pettit, Michael Steinke, Neil Dalleywater, Rikki James, Richard Kimbrough, Kevin Jones, Jochen Brauer, the Gerrard family, Miles Newman, Simon Holloway, Helmut and Nelly Oberlander, Richard and Amanda Ligato, Mark Walker, Ruben Horemans, Jerry Jess, Onkel Gunnar, Stan Wohlfarth, Jim DiGennaro, Fred Crellin, Matt Keene, Ian Nankervis, Ian Lloyd, Andy Tindale, Andreas Plogmaker, Mike Howles, Ben Hayes, Brian Ford, Stephen Hughes, Neil Smart, Lyndsay Rowe, Frank Meels, Bootscooter, Mike Brooks, Kelly Lewis, Liz Gundy, Christian Christensen, David Dirk, Bryan Gregg, Jenni Gemmell, Andrew Fowler, Sam Carter, Isaiah Hanback, Ben Bosworth's family, Christian Figenschou, David B and Matt Smith.

Thanks also to all those owners whose stories we are privileged to retell and who took time to talk to us and look through their family photo archives. In particular we would like to thank:

Cris Torlasco for organising pictures and writing text for the Oberlanders' story.
Richard and Amanda Ligato for permission to print extracts from their book *Wide Eyed Wanderers*.
Jacob Devaney for background information on Bessie.
Bob van Heyst for organising pictures of the Flower Power Bus.
Lisa Guthrie for information about the Guthrie Walk.
Kevin Jones for permission to print an extract from his book *Inshallah*.
Dr Bob Hieronimus for pictures and information about the Light Bus.
Richard Kimbrough for pictures and information about the Shasta Snow Trip.
Christian Figenschou for sharing his story and pictures about crossing Africa.
VW VAG for archive material.
Volkswagen Camper and Commercial magazine.

Page 79: photograph © Empics
Page 134 far left and page 138: photographs © bigpicturesphoto.com